No Apocalypse, No Integration

Post-Contemporary Interventions

Series Editors: Stanley Fish and

Fredric Jameson

A Book in the Series

Latin America in Translation

en Traducción

em Tradução

Sponsored by the Duke-

University of North Carolina

Program in Latin American Studies

NO APOCALYPSE, NO INTEGRATION

Modernism and Postmodernism in Latin America

Martín Hopenhayn

Translated by Cynthia Margarita Tompkins

and Elizabeth Rosa Horan

Duke University Press   Durham and London 2001

© 2001 Duke University Press

All rights reserved

Printed in the United States of America on acid-free paper ∞

Typeset in Galliard by Keystone Typesetting, Inc.

Library of Congress Cataloging-in-Publication Data appear

on the last printed page of this book.

Contents

Preface to the Spanish Edition   vii

Preface to the English Edition   xi

1   The Day after the Death of a Revolution   1

2   Disenchanted and Triumphant toward the 21st Century:
    A Prospect of Cultural Moods in South America   13

3   Neither Apocalyptic nor Integrated
    (Eight Debatable Paradoxes)   36

4   Realism and Revolt, Twenty Years Later
    (Paris 1968–Santiago de Chile 1988)   47

5   What is Left Positive from Negative Thought?
    A Latin American Perspective   55

6   Postmodernism and Neoliberalism in Latin America   77

7   The Crisis of Legitimacy of the Planning State   94

8   Is the Social Thinkable without Metanarratives?   119

9   Utopia against Crisis, or How to Awake from a Long Insomnia   142

    Index   155

Preface to the Spanish Edition

A thread, tough and slender, runs through the following pages.

It's not the thread of disenchantment. What I mean is that the collective dreams that gave way to the rigors of history ask the survivors not to give way, in turn, to the temptation of the usual litany. Such laments might be lucid, yet avoiding them could be the most sensible way of mourning these corpse-like histories. Despite their rubble, these histories extended much, all-too-human hope.

Nor is this the thread of euphoric amnesia, which has proclaimed the end of hard times and the coming of the *soft and cool* paradise. I don't deny that it's healthy to forget, when doing so refreshes thinking and liberates new, constructive drives. But the form in which forgetting tends to be invoked these days, in the wake of its invitation to plasticity and liberty, reeks of the consecration of injustice.

The thread need be tough then, and slender, very fine, doubled, to unite these pages since the speed (and not the collapse) of the times makes the grave-digger a midwife and vice-versa. The thread needs to establish what is irrecoverable and, in a single operation, size up what can be recycled.

If some myths of emancipation or development seem to have shattered into a thousand pieces — as much in Latin America as in other regions — fragments of those myths will always remain. Such shards and tatters furnish part of the raw material for elaborating new collective projects.

But the ambiguity doesn't end there. Social condition and existence may seem damned by the absence of a motivating narrative, yet they are never totally deprived of hope. There is always reason to debate alternatives, be they simulacra of promise, rituals of anticipation or constructive theory. Of course social existence in this part of the world has never been easy. Indeed, it's always been full of voluptuous nuances. Ethical complexity and expressive richness live together in our social ties, inhabiting our embraces and aggressions. This ambivalence in sociability reappears under new figures. Grassroots communities live side by side with postmodern tribes of urban youth; the expression of violence in the large cities combines with the call for greater participation on the part of citizens, and the demand for greater political transparency coexists with politics turned into televised spectacle or show business.

The essays contained in this volume look to capture these new forms of ambiguity, to establish the breaks but above all the threads, tough and slender, that crisscross the gaps, that go through fire, not emerging intact, but not totally disintegrating either. Such is the leitmotiv here: break and re-creation in Latin American sociability.

In what tones is this song sung? The reader might find the following references worthwhile in pondering the theoretical range that the following pages travel.

The reevaluation and recomposition of the cultural dimension of development shows a more than anthropological, almost metaphysical respect for the symbolic; an unprecedented popularity of stories regarding our heterogeneity and diversity; an enthusiastic reconsideration of indigenous, rural tradition and of furious urban rockers; a broad consensus with regard to the necessity of considering the cultural variable in development proposals and discourse.

There's a compulsive equation that identifies secular common sense with the spirit of the private. Its most disquieting symptom, complacency about the fever for economic privatization, contrasts with endogenous impulses toward communitarianism, mythic thought, moral traditionalism, popular religiosity, and millenary customs. These premodern impulses are either excluded from or absorbed by privatist secularization.

In the almost unanimous exaltation of political democratization as an institutional requisite for actualizing old emancipatory ideals there is a desire, *by way of democracy,* to open a flank where personal and group dreams might have public visibility. This is coupled with the defense of institutional democracy as the order of "life" against exclusion, authoritarianism and the cultures of death.

From the day-to-day recovery of the logic and strategies of social movements, grassroots organizations, counter cultures, and popular expressions of resistance there appears, in the end, a curiosity with regard to peripheral conditions and existence. These are no longer present as folklore but as the rule of partial, even tribal spaces where ideals of autonomy, participation, and the development of human potential enter into play.

Amid the massive suspicion regarding great ideals appears a truly massive loss of belief in large-scale projects, collective stories, and societal utopias. This suspicion arises together with an urgency to counter the new waves of political pragmatism and individual cynicism, by way of illusions and proposals infused with new content, perhaps with greater humility and fewer pretensions than the previous utopias, but not ineffective for this.

A consequence of the worldwide eruption of a rational delirium is that the speed of operations, inversions, reconversions, ramifications, renovations, incorporations, speculations, and tides has increased exponentially, beyond human grasp, far beyond any kind of voluntary control. Any centralized effort at imposing order would be interpreted as suicidal.

And at the same time — or as part of the same — we're confronted with the multiplication of options for integrating or marginalizing ourselves, with software for all tastes and all perversions, and with the temptation to reconstruct ourselves (cybernetically, computationally, telecommunicationally) freed of the weightiness of being. It's as if we could get rid of thinking for ourselves by devotedly or playfully appropriating technology, if we set all of our intelligence towards nourishing the euphoria of this techno-wave that can really irritate us when we're in a bad mood.

These pages observe a postmodern disenchantment with ideals such as the constitution of the subject, progress as the engine that drives history, the encyclopedic and academic tendencies of the highly literate, the tendency towards a kind of teleology in the social sciences, the commitment to systemic change — ultimately, everything that finished by making us ineffective because we wanted to be absolutely consistent.

The delegitimation of the State as the propeller of development and the builder of society likewise shapes these pages. With that delegitimation comes the subsequent loss of prestige and influence for normative state planning and of revolutionary strategy. These no longer provide the link between political action and social reflection. They are no longer convincing with regard to creating a nexus between science and progress. They have lost support, in the street as in the universities, the parliament, and literature.

These are crises of enlightened reason, utopian reason, historical reason. The crisis of reason would be understood, just like that, as modern reason, but also as modernity embodied in the patterns and discourses of modernization in Latin America. Crisis as inflection, a place for the new, a metamorphosis of the spirit of a new epoch.

The essays that follow wish to put pressure on that spirit that wavers between agony and transfiguration. Under the pressure of new, hypercontemporary secularization, *lo nuestro*, "our own," seeks to materialize as renewed identity. That identity combines the expectation of superconnection with the menace of loss.

How to resignify the collective future, beyond the invocation to democratic coexistence? From what point or place to rethink the imaginary-but-tense link that unites subjectivity with power? What happens to the drive to freedom once the stories that crystallize it have died? These questions have been resonating for a good many years now, in Latin America. Their answers, luckily, are not univocal: they puff through these pages precisely because of the ambivalence that they provoke.

The texts that follow this preface are generational, almost excessively so. Here is a slender thread that touches on new forms of narrating the spirit of a lost generation of Latin Americans that arrived late to the epic of the 60s and that managed to breathe the stale hangover of that era, subsequently becoming disenchanted and fearful, without resigning itself to cynicism or nihilism at the century's end. It is a generation that reclaims the act of dreaming despite or because of the radical depopulation of collective dreams. But at the same time it claims that right without too much shouting or resorting to violence, be it for an aesthetic rejection of bad taste, a phantasmagoric fear of chaos, or a more concrete fear of losing a job.

This is a text, all in all, that would like to raise public consciousness and, from this end-of-the-millennium collapse, to insinuate a profile emerging from the ruins. Most of all, it would like to bear witness to the many deaths of God occurring in such short time.

Preface to the English Edition

The essays constituting this book are variations on a pair of questions. What are the outward forms of the crisis of modernity in the Latin American periphery? In a continent marked by thwarted modernization, new waves of privatization, the exclusion of great masses of people and profound sociocultural heterogeneity, how is the postmodern criticism of Enlightenment and Utopianism understood?

Such is the context for the texts that follow. They deal with three profound crises that have shaken Latin America since the onset of the 1980s, crises that are the foundation of its incomplete or poorly resolved incorporation into modernity. There is the crisis of utopias, especially the socialist utopia, which promised to deliver social change. There is the crisis of state modernization and development discourse, operating from the end of World War II until the end of the 1960s. These crises feed yet another, concerning the role of the social sciences and intellectuals.

The object of this preface is to present an overview of each of these crises. Drawing ideas from the texts comprising this edition, this preface aims to familiarize the reader with the subjects under consideration.

The Crisis of Utopias Promising Social Change

The promise of revolution (socialist, nationalist, anti-imperialist) contributed to the prospect of radical change within the collective consciousness of Latin America. This prospect or hope proposed that intense social mobilization and political struggle would offer future redemption from social injustice, poverty, exclusion, external dependency, and capitalist alienation. There is no country on the continent that did not at some point in time internalize this image of the possible future, which transformed the bounds and appearances of political discourse, mingling with the "dance of the symbols" already afloat in diverse Latin American societies. While enlightened readers understood the promise of the socialist revolution as historically necessary, the popular sectors seized that promise as a clear-cut hope for liberation. Redemption through massive social change, the end of hard times, and the coming of the kingdom of the poor entered into the popular imaginary. Images of general resurrection, with wagon loads of pilgrims pouring into unprecedented rallies, and divine justice descending to distribute goods, produced an almost drunken giddiness in leftist intellectuals as well as ordinary folk. Political discourse was rearticulated, as was the ideology of progress and art, in a dialectic like that of a Greek chorus in which the tragic hero was very much a messiah. That messiah had various names: Che Guevara, Camilo Torres, Salvador Allende.

But these expectations of liberation and redemption were violently frustrated. The political defeat of the left and of "progressive movements" during the 1970s, as well as the delegitimation of socialism and development discourse in the 1980s, left national societies bereft of utopias. For society, the erasure from the future, from even the insubstantial realm of hope, of the image of social change along with prospects for liberation from poverty and alienation, constitutes a form of death and of cultural transfiguration.

The collapse of true socialist governments, the hard apprenticeships under the dictatorships, the overthrow of Ortega in Nicaragua and the deterioration of the image of Fidel's regime in Cuba, along with the rationalization of markets and the triumph of pragmatists in the political arena, brought the strength of the utopian images to an end, so that intellectuals were left without a committed science, militants without a vital cause, and the marginalized, more alone than ever.

Explanations for the defeat of the great utopias of social change abound. More provocative are the questions regarding the possibility of new plans for liberation. What is happening today with that mass of energy that came together to support the socialist wager; where is that energy headed today? Does it make sense to seek new roads toward integration, new syntheses between personal desire and large-scale projets, ultimately seeking a new dialectic which puts alienation aside, affirming liberty and justice?*

The defeat of the revolutionary or egalitarian utopia entails a search for alternative forms of gratification and self-affirmation. Facing a future in which the fleshed-out image of social revolution has lost the appearance of truth, liberating energies dissipate in a cloud of alternatives that don't add up to a single project or total discourse. Rather, they bring to society the fresh air of new searches: popular religious feeling, grass roots movements, diversified consumption in the growing cultural industry, adhesion to a broad menu of esoteric doctrines and programs for personal development, identification with small groups that call for citizens' solidarity, struggles to expand democracy in limited, local spaces, the "postmodern tribalization" of urban youth. These and other dynamics summarize the dispersed energy, deprived of utopias, that thirsts for meaning.

These alternatives did not emerge as the reformulation of a great historical synthesis, but rather, as diverse forms of expression and smaller cooperative projects. Emerging from this framework are values such as pluralism, respect for differences, and the exaltation of diversity. Shall these values be the stuff of a new discourse of liberation?

The Crisis of State Modernization and Development Discourse

The mid-1970s signaled the irruption of various phenomena which would have a devastating effect on the state-centered development paradigm that had dominated Latin America from the postwar period to the early 1980s economic crisis. Standing out among these phenomena are the growth, within post-industrial capitalism, of "financial" (as opposed to "productive") capitalism, the stagnation of national economies, the crisis of legit-

---

*On "integration," see Umberto Eco's *Apocalípticos e integrados ante la cultura de masas* (Spain: Editorial Lumen, 1965); however, Eco's work is more closely tied to the culture industry and its impact on mass culture. To some extent my work's use of these terms "apocalyptic" or "integrated" includes Eco's work, but in a broader sense. That is, "apocalyptic" not only refers to those who regard mass culture as alienating, but to those who regard the so-called "end of utopias" with a postmodern fatalism, who feel that globalization represents the triumph of raw, unbridled neo-liberalism. The "integrated" refers not

imacy facing the political system of state-driven development, and the new orientations proposed by the political economists known in our continent under the archetypal figure of the "Chicago Boys."

All these phenomena have undermined the legitimacy of the so-called "development policy" of the preceding decades. The paradigmatic formulation known as "the import substitution model" is attributed to CEPAL (the Economic Commission for Latin America and the Caribbean). More than an institutional or academic artifact, development policy was a synthesis coined from historical experience. Its objective, which had always enjoyed political, technical, and social consensus, was to accelerate the movement of societies and national economies towards higher levels of development and industrialization. State development policy kept this future in mind as it tried to reach a series of objectives required for accelerated modernization. These objectives included the promotion and diversification of domestic industry; the expansion of internal markets; the modernization of human resources and agrarian economy; economic stability and growth; and social integration by way of modernized labor, educational expansion, urbanization, and access to basic services.

The substitution of domestic products for imports turned out to possess less integrative capacity than originally imagined. The problem owed as much to domestic deficiencies as to exogenous forces. It also produced corrosive effects: in the name of modernization it destroyed the cultural roots of sectors that were marginalized and excluded from development even as those now-informal sectors adopted the expectations of an industrial culture. But these deficiencies or trade-offs in the model did not require a consecration of the neoliberal prescription, which had no remedy for the dynamic deficiencies of this "peripheral capitalism" (which CEPAL had forewarned for quite some time). Nor did neoliberal prescriptions remedy the economic growth without social equity that has charac-

---

only to those who can participate in mass culture and the consumption of media icons but also to those who reap the benefits of the Third Industrial Revolution, those who are comfortable with the new style of "possessive individualism" that characterizes neoliberalism's new sensitivity and who share the consumerist aspirations that are induced by commercial globalization. The fact that this book is titled *No Apocalypse, No Integration* is an echo of Eco, or an anti-Eco. The idea is that it's no longer easy to locate oneself in one or another of the two trenches, of the apocalyptic or of the integrated. Rather, the majority participates in various mediations and intermediary strategies between the two.

terized our countries even in times of shared enthusiasm with respect to the modernizing paradigm.

The crisis in the state development model has forced a revision of the role of the State in Latin American societies, for this model was always associated with an ideal of the State as driving the economy and constructing the actors of development. So-called "State Planning" in Latin America has been decreasing for some time, eroded from many sides. Among the objections to this Demiurgic State — driving force of modernization, impartial arbitrator of social conflicts and great political totalizer — are that it is both utopian and formalist, erratic and rigid, capitalist and an obstacle to capitalism, vulnerable and hypertrophied. Its very conception is considered to have been an error, illusion, or failure. The crisis of the 1980s (with the following decade lost to development) effectively killed a project that was, until the 1970s, still the functional formula for mixed (half-state, half-private) economies. The development model was attacked by the new right and by the new left, by ideology and economics (and ideology packaged in economics), by politics and by culture.

The defeat of the model of development based on the substitution of domestic goods for imports and on State Planning created a huge gap, an open space into which neoliberal offensives have rushed in to promote the hegemonic ideology of the strong market. This is an ideology that runs through politics, the sensitivity of the intelligentsia, and the mass media. The gap nonetheless created an opening for alternative proposals and perceptions. The revalorization of democracy in a post-ideological context has enabled new topics for political debate. These include the diversity of cultures and of values, concern for greater equity in opportunities for professional and personal development, and the construction of more representative channels for processing social demands in the political system. The enhancement of democratic governability in situations of social fragmentation brings with it the decentralization of public management. With change in political economies comes the more democratic and participatory use of the growing culture industry. Sooner or later those topics should acquire greater prominence in national debate within Latin American countries.

It's also worth noting, in this sense, the emergence of social movements as bearers of new forms of political practice. The crisis of legitimacy in the party system and of the Centralist State has given way to a new search for political renewal. Within this framework, social movements appear as the most direct and democratic alternative for processing demands. Attributed to them is the ability to express collective identities in public spaces, and to better represent people's real interests. On another plane, new social movements have been considered as embryos of alternative socialization. New understandings of shared identity, greater cooperative participation, and greater democratization of social life and local spaces spring from them. While pondering the influence of new social movements on the construction of political consciousness is no easy task, their emergence poses a motivating challenge, one that calls for the rescue of popular creativity and for alternative development discourses.

Those who once shared enthusiasm for state development policy and are now searching for alternatives to the status quo are asking themselves: in what measure can social movements, political heterodoxy, and the expansive impulse of democracy serve as a base for a different, more just, more appropriate model? And in what measure can dispersed energies come together to call for questions, in political and cultural terms, to interpellate that status quo?

Crisis among Intellectuals and Social Scientists

The destiny of the "intelligentsia" and of the Latin American social sciences was strongly conditioned by theories of social change. Most intellectuals and social scientists were seen, over the decades, as closely committed to development discourse and to the leftist agenda of a possible revolution. It is not strange, then, that the crisis of state development policy and the failure of the socialist wager on revolution would have an especially strong impact on the figure of the intellectual and the social scientist.

This book offers insights into the consequences of this impact. It gauges the transition presently running through the social sciences and "well-read" social thought. The political defeats, which overthrew the enlightened pretensions of social science, have left social scientists and intellectuals in an impasse marked by a double crisis: of "intelligibility" and of "organicity."

By the crisis of intelligibility I refer to the difficulties that critical social thought has experienced in attempting to grasp the new political, cultural, and social scenarios that have emerged on the Latin American map. The interpretive capacity of the social sciences was overwhelmed by the hegemony of neoliberalism, the complexity of the social fabric, and the exhausting effects of the culture industry. Comprehensive structural explanations of reality were overtaken by scenarios requiring new, more heterodox, nuanced readings. Perplexity was making itself more evident in the figure of the social scientist to whom, until recently, was attributed the power of reading and extracting from history the last word in explanations. This is clearly shown in the loss of relevance of the three most significant paradigms dominating social scientific practice from the 1950s to the 1970s in Latin America: "CEPAL-ism"[1] (or development policy in its "original" meaning), orthodox Marxism, and the paradigm of the so-called "dependency theorists."

The crisis of organicity involves breaking the link between knowledge production and practical intervention. This break is very significant, since the social scientist and the intellectual have, for various decades, justified their roles, to others and to themselves, as a function of their practical contribution to social change. The political and cultural defeat of the left, plus the political and technical defeat of development policy and its national variants, dismantled the Latin American social sciences' greatest source of legitimacy, which was its claim to the organic (or supposedly organic) articulation between knowledge production and the radical transformation of social structures.

One need not be postmodern to understand the exaggeration with which the Western Enlightenment, matrix of the producer of knowledge was incarnate in the model of the Latin American social scientist as modern, progressive, and endowed with an almost mythical ability. Capable of deciphering the nature of reason, the model social scientist would then identify the rational movement of history, and finally use reason to recognize the best future direction. Certainly one need not resort to the anti-utopian discourse of disenchantment in order to feel the psychological and even spiritual costs imposed when the image of a possible revolution was ground into dust. Even if that revolution were to be situated in some uncertain future, as an image, it has definitively lost its force for mobilizing the masses; as a discourse, it has lost the appearance of reality.

Casting doubt on the great projects of modernization previously constituting the basic material of political-symbolic consumption in Latin America (whether in terms of national development or in socialist terms) moves intellectuals and social scientists to wonder about how their own knowledge production contributes to future social and political change. On the other hand, disenchantment and the lack of confidence generated by political failures and the discrediting of paradigms of social interpretation lead to much higher stakes of heterodoxy in the means of grasping reality. The result is that it becomes difficult to define current boundaries between heterodoxy and eclecticism in the Latin American social scientist's interpretive practice. As a result of the need to resort to tools from distinct analytical currents, and the abandonment of globalizing categories nourished by strong ideologies, theory has been exposed to the most hybrid formulations.

How to exercise social criticism in Latin America today? What could its objectives be, avoiding self-pitying pessimism or paralyzing fatalism? Is it possible to uncover a mode of reflection for suggesting and rescuing new liberating features in social reality, to create a space for hopes oriented towards a more humanized order, to promote a more affirmative and less heteronomous culture?

The current options would seem to indicate new mediations between the social scientist and the scientist's object, between the intellectual and reality. A bit of Enlightenment and Utopianism is needed to counterbalance the overly pragmatic and functionalist bias that threatens to co-opt the production of knowledge, or to limit the uncritical apologies for the virtues of the market. It is necessary to delve into society's cultural production, into new life strategies, into the irreducible cultural mixing that subsists and survives in Latin America. It is necessary to speak in the plural, in terms of perspectives and alternative scenarios, to be more humble in the transmission of knowledge, but more adventurous in experimenting with that knowledge. To carry the value of pluralism from political to epistemological options, to be pluralist as social scientists. To modify forms as well as contents, personal attitude as well as object. To convert oneself, for a time, into the very object of investigation, to immerse oneself in the very emotions of disenchantment and personal perplexity, of one's neighbors and equals. To discard nothing as irrational or irrelevant. To behold, from close up, the new hues and profiles of collective identity, the features of sensibility and of personality, such as never occurred to a development policy planner or scientist of the revolution.

The disenchantment that succeeds perplexity in these crises has two faces: entropy and alchemy. The former paralyzes and undermines the creative imagination. The latter accepts failure as an opportunity for conceiving new forms of utopian invention and libertarian mysticism. The author of the present book looks at the second face, not in order to give answers, but to stir up the embers of the search-fires.

Note

1   The term CEPAL-ism refers to the development strategies proposed by CEPAL-ECLAC (*Comisión Económica para América Latina y el Caribe,* Economic Commission for Latin America and the Caribbean) in the 1950s and 1960s. These strategies are based on accelerated industrialization, import substitution and the stimulation of domestic demand, with the strong participation of the State in economic action.

No Apocalypse, No Integration

1 ❋ The Day after the Death of a Revolution

We are, without doubt, crossed by interwoven uncertainties. These uncertainties are reflected in expressions such as the crisis of the Welfare State (and its Latin American variant, the Planning State), and the loss of the centrality of class struggle to the historical imagination. In expressions such as the new dependency, in our experience of social and cultural fragmentation, in our disenchantment facing a humbled economy and a humble democracy, we awake as if from a pleasant dream—and why not, possibly from a nightmare too—called revolution. All of these expressions contribute to the moral atmosphere of doubt. Facing them, doubt nags away at us: are we still looking for some form of totalization, for a new comprehensive explanation, for another subject hearkening to the universal, for an unprecedented and inevitably energizing impulse toward utopia? There exists, of course, a strong reservation facing the prospect or hope that political renovation or sustained modernization would re-motivate a fantasized historical synthesis. What the societies of Latin America most share today are social deterioration, formal democracy, privatizing euphoria and shock politics. These terse coincidences can hardly be said to constitute the raw material for meaningful emancipation, for creating a future and for absorbing the dormant memory of the "people."

In view of the above, the following pages might seem skeptical. They don't indicate new avenues for change nor do they revitalize old impulses for radical transformation. Rather, they trace the crisis and the consequences following the shattered dream of integration. The shattering of that dream has profoundly affected culture, daily life, and the pursuit of happiness.

Culture Ablaze

If the revolution were imagined in social terms as a hot blaze in which the basic structures of dependency capitalism were to be consumed and regress to an earlier stage, we would now confront the congealed ashes of the very idea of revolution. It's more than just a question of political, strategic, or ideological turnarounds. To abandon the image of a possible revolution is a cultural mutation, a peculiar way to die.

To die for the lack of events. The revolution was conceived as moment and *momentum,* when history would fall apart through conscious and collective action, an inflection and change of course toward the foundational appropriation of the present. Without revolution, we're left without the emotion of the great event.

To die for the lack of redemption. The revolution, while made by a few, would redeem all of us from capitalist alienation, from the small and muffled dramas of bourgeois individualism, and from the viscous contamination of exploitation. Party or proletariat were seen as particular subjects, with the ability to act as pivots, to make universal emancipation turn around. Our doubts and shames would be left behind. Without a revolution, we've no choice but to put up with them.

To die for the lack of fusion. The image of a possible, meaningful revolution supposed the full integration of personal with communal life. The seamless communion of one's life projects with one's world project provided the rounded, succinct justification of one's own, personal existence. The image of oneself tossed out into the street, fused into a seething mass that lays waste to all vestiges of an order verging on decay, could prove almost ecstatic.

With no prospects of revolution, present life loses its epic potential. This would lead to a range of consequences, among which it would be useful to single out the ones that most contribute to a culture of disenchantment and chilliness of temperament.

In the first place, there's the necessity of remaking and resignifying[1] personal existence. That existence was previously based on a sum of "minor reasons" that never constituted a "total reason." Even so, those "reasons" somehow managed to conjure, partially, temporarily, the loss of the earlier metahistorical referent. Almost without realizing it we substitute the single program for a collection of "software" that we select depending on the occasion: the software of personal growth, of political pragmatism, of career advancement, of social recognition, of moral transgressions. For lack of coherence, we replace the emphasis on the substantive with the satisfaction of style. Some of us adhere to some small scale, minor caliber collective projects. The word "individualist" no longer strikes us as sinful; it has become more musical than the word "collectivist."

In the second place, we pass from the utopian thinking to the *ad hoc*. The lack of a final condition of total reconciliation has led us to constant readjustment, using strategies not as the means to achieve a glorious end, but as the end in itself. Even in politics, form has become content. If the image of revolutionary action may be seen against a clear and distant horizon, in the absence of that image, vision tends to settle for minimal, short term change, regression into the interstices, the spaces in between. The lack of utopias is not only the dissolution of dreams, but also the perpetuation of a drowsy, pointillist insomnia.

In the third place, we've renounced the wish to break away. Previously, the categorical imperative could always be found in a necessary assassination, real or symbolic, of the bourgeois, capitalist, or imperialist. Today we toy with these figures, justifying ourselves through them, and, at most, joking around with them in nocturnal rituals or waking fantasies. The verb "to break" has lost its once irresistible charm, its once implicit violence as a verb that could be sheathed in beauty: Fanon, Guevara and Ho Chi Minh were the very examples of this aestheticization of violence. The mere inevitability of a radical break constituted a relief, in and of itself. Now it's all too clear that this is less inevitable than it once seemed.

In the fourth place, socialism no longer appears as the possibility of social synthesis or full integration between State and society. This means accepting two divergent perspectives: we're induced to recognize social fragmentation as an inexorable reality, or to accept a new kind of totalization, the result of the transnationalization of the economy and the rearticulative impact of new technologies and the flourishing cultural industry. We nonetheless know that both interpretations, both perspectives, can be one and the same: until now, the remapping, in global terms, of the international economic scenario has heightened the processes of social fragmentation already evidenced by the styles of development promoted in Latin America over the past three or four decades, consecrating a status quo where the (internationally) integrated are starkly juxtaposed with the (nationally) excluded. The alternative to these possibilities has so far been unspecified stammering about "endogenous development." The development alternatives are likely to be reduced to appeals to vague principle or molecular integration that turn the actors into great heroes to themselves and little monads to the rest.

Ultimately, the recomposition of the worldwide economic system and the globalization of communications provokes an accelerated deterritorialization, which makes it very difficult to maintain a stable identity associated with the territory in which one lives and the nation to which one belongs. It's not easy to evaluate the impact on collective projects of phenomena such as the relocation of productive activities beyond the countries' borders, planet-wide simultaneity in the interchange of information, and the displacement — at the speed of light and with uncontrollable destinations — of the symbolic products of local origin. On television screens, identities jumble together in a worldwide dance of mutant, rapidly obsolescent symbols. The globalization of markets and communications provokes a growing permeability and a *porosity of imaginaries* that nobody could rationalize. Expressed as a caricature, the currently reigning ideology can last as long as a commercial announcement or an ethnographic program on the television.

Following the revolution's diluted horizons and the broken promises of sustained modernization's integrative potential (for it failed to integrate as expected, even when it was effectively sustained), questions about the *meaning* and *axis* of the continent's present history become difficult even to formulate. Beyond political viability or will, it's a question of what is — or is not — culturally possible: the pulverization of large-scale projects, the loss of conviction in homogenous, universally beneficent progress, the turn towards seeking shelter in life's small business, exchanging the substantive for the procedural in our symbolic order, the inability to imagine radical change or large-scale initiatives, a certain complacency towards discontinuity and fragmentation in all walks of sociocultural life, and finally, the preeminence of a kind of exclusionary transnationalization that is neither national nor popular. Don't these circumstances make it difficult even to think of roads to development that might seduce and mobilize our old and new masses? From what utopia, or with what ends in mind, is the epic of history conceivable once the bonfire of revolutionary dreaming is quenched, along with the spectacle of mass liberation and the promise of sustained progress?[2]

The Smouldering Ashes of the Everyday

Devoid of the Great Project, the everyday turns into what it is: the life of each and all days. Healthy minimalism? Maybe so. We all have our little projects, filling up and justifying the day, the week, the month, the year at most. Academics, with their research projects, organizers with their action projects, members of the informal sector with their community development projects, political activists with their realist projects, yuppies with their fortunate transactions. The old utopian Great Project turns into these smaller missions that are disseminated by way of programs, initiatives that are born and die: local proposals. None of them last very long, yet the multiple possibilities and effects of that underlying initiative are inscribed everywhere and in everything. Shall we sing an elegy or spell out an apology for the discontinuity that we all endure in the day-to-day? A bit of each, mixed up and turned around.

How is an everyday life constituted and made meaningful when it's characterized by the little project and discontinuity, in a sequence of juxtaposed routines that don't necessarily add up to a whole? How to think of a process of integration along the macro-scale, when even the micro-scale seems incapable of integration? Maybe it would be a kind of integration which replaces meaning with the *administration* of the diverse, merely a matter of control and of defining boundaries.

It's no coincidence that ever since the death of the image of the revolution (with its beatific mode of integration and universalist vocation), everyday life in Latin America has been increasingly studied. There's a growing attempt to find, in the porosity of that molecular life, the discreet charm of possible rites, latent magic, booming identities. It's quite clear that the everyday becomes the natural repository for expectations that have had to abandon the pasturelands of total liberation. It's in this private terrain that postmoderns, for example, want to find a field for ongoing experiment and a ludic passage between fashions, languages, and expressions throughout time. Does the play of forms substitute for modernizing or revolutionary integration?

Surely all of this suggests a vision of the everyday as permanently and doubly marked. On the one hand, the rich diversity of experience, but also the exasperating evidence of non-transcendence. On the other hand, ashes, nothing solid built on them, although they're soft and fresh to the end. Such is the dual face of the superficial creativity and underlying hybridity.

Doubtless, everyday life is not the same for everyone. Today more than ever, Latin America demonstrates a fundamental divide that cuts through even its tiniest routines. It is the divide of social contrasts. In absolute numbers there are more impoverished people today than there were a decade ago, and the distribution of income is less equitable than at the beginning of the 80s. Curiously, the end of the dream of revolution is produced in circumstances in which the contradictions that previously made the revolution (or structural change) a totalizing, inescapable event now appear more acute, while social injustice and dependency are greater and more dramatic than ever. In vast sectors of the population, the gap between expectations for consumption and the impossibility of filling them is an ever-widening one. It's not for nothing that violence has entered in, as an everyday reality, in many a Latin American metropolis. No longer can this violence be moralized as revolutionary violence or reduced to the counter-expression of an exclusionary model of development. It gains increasingly in public visibility.

For the sectors excluded from development, the insecurity of existence is an everyday occurrence: physical insecurity in the big cities, job insecurity, insecurity with respect to income and promised-but-frustrated social mobility. All these factors bring with them a sense of the everyday in which life turns into a fragile thing. Even the body itself can be experienced as an object of dubious strength. The *uncertainty effect* becomes a climate.

In contrast to the insecurity of the excluded, those who are integrated experience the everyday dimension of life through progressive diversification by way of consumerism and a swift incorporation of the latest technological advantages. In the social strata of the so-called fortunate, the everyday is populated by new services, the exotic stuff of science fiction, and a certain spirit of *cool* in using and acquiring new goods and services. The possibility of information technology and telecommunication facilitates permanent connection to the world, unlimited access to information, and diversified exchange with diverse peers. So is everyday life networked, and those who benefit from development increasingly reach a perfect mutual understanding. This leads to a ceaseless mobility of receivers and emissors, to a vertigo-inducing, ever-changing cross-talk among rotating subjects, and to an accelerated innovation in the manipulation of objects and communication between subjects. Here, the *provisional effect* becomes a climate.

What's precarious for some is temporary for others.[3] The former, lived as a drama without any prospect of resolution. The latter, a slight commitment aired out and set afloat. In Brazil, for example, the world's fourth largest transnational television network coexists with 19 percent illiteracy and millions of children living in the streets. Of course, heterogeneity crosses the uncertain as much as the provisional. For the excluded, heterogeneity appears under the form of an astounding proliferation of roles for surviving and strategies for not succumbing, and of continual displacement from one strategy to another. For the integrated, heterogeneity appears in the diversified consumption of objects, in the use of services and of kinds of investments, and in the connection with a greater variety of peers. But everyday life recomposes itself, whether in terms of imposed uncertainty or as a chosen provisionality. This de-centering allows the inference, even if only by way of speculation, of the following effects:

1. It isn't all that easy, anymore, to associate *the everyday* with *continuity*. Uncertain or a provisional existence causes the everyday to lose some of its character of "progressive excavation." It loses depth and grows wider. The material of the everyday becomes more random, less predictable, less readily planned. The flexibility of images, codes, languages, and rules in the new industrial-cultural complex also permeates everyday life, giving rise to an ongoing metamorphosis of images, symbols, and traditions. This becomes more contingent than ever in a world eternally reinventing itself on a diskette or on a video-game tape.

2. The reiterative dimension of the everyday, may not, by definition, disappear, but it can at the least become attenuated. It's no longer that easy to see the everyday as the substrata of repetition that prolongs us, in a circular fashion, through time and across space. Insecurity in employment contributes to this by forcing a more intense circle of work activities. Other factors include the acceleration of technical change, with its effects in productive routines and in objects and services that are consumed; the volubility of familiar roles, whether on account of cultural changes or pressures to survive; and the recomposition of the economic scene, in

which accumulation rests less in the continuity of a business than in a certain "sense of opportunity." Nothing seems to be repeated anymore. Everything is recreated and reprogrammed without pause in the all-embracing language of computing and in the communicative extroversion of the mass media. The transvestism observable in new cultural markets suggests to us that the everyday is no longer repetition, but a series of removes. It ceases to provide a circular substratum to time.

3. Owing to the preceding, the importance of speed for everyday life is greater today than ever before, in order to survive, to progress, to be informed, and to capitalize on all additional advances brought about by way of technical supplies.

4. The short term has become the permanent, total horizon of daily life, as much through uncertainty in some and provisionality in others, as for the acceleration of change in all walks of everyday life. This might appear to be a characteristic innate to the field of the everyday, which is, in the long run, the field of the immediate. Nonetheless, it's not the same thing to live the immediate towards a horizon felt to be for the long term as to experience it as a horizon in and of itself.

Finally, minimalism has been converted into a well-regarded value for daily action. All big projects are dismissed as pretentious or unrealistic. The value attributed to nuance, detail, and the circumstantial returns. This minimalism is fleshed out in the logic of software, which each person creates or interchanges according to preference, situations, or objects, and where there is no horizon other than the moment's required operation.

In synthesis, the everyday comes marked by the signs of decreased continuity and repetition, by increased speed and an exacerbation of the short term, plus a certain minimalist complacency. All of this intersects with the double face of the social, involving the uncertain and the provisional, the forced and the chosen, the excluded and the integrated.

Once again, the unanswered question: How, with these aspects of the everyday, to conceive an idea that will effectively spur eventual collective emancipation? How to do so from the revival of individualism, discontinuity, uncertainty, and the provisional quality of daily life? How to do so considering the fugacity of social ties, superficial creativity and underlying hybridity, the institutionalization of violence, the inability to predict, the difficulty of planning, the pathos of fragility and insecurity, the exaltation (or lament) of the ephemeral, the loss of social sensibility, the abdication of the middle and long term speed and the solidification of minimalism as norm and value? Which raw material of everyday life is open to becoming a unifying material for historical life?

Life's Cool Joy

How does this difficulty of integration—a difficulty translated into minimal dreams, pulverized utopias—intersect and modify the forms in which we procure life's joy? In what manner do the new signs of everyday life and sensitivity intersect with consciousness' bent toward happiness?

Can one speak of a *lesser* disposition to life's joy, through the workings of conditions such as the death of a redeeming utopia (with its subjective consequences), greater socio-cultural fragmentation, and the renunciation of integration by way of modernizing development? Is it possible to think that one may take greater joy in life, thanks to the return to individualism, the increased weightlessness that discontinuity offers, the small but more frequent achievements that minimalism dispenses, and the aestheticizing spectacle of diversity? What promise to the ecstasy of body and spirit is inaugurated through the virtual images that seemingly offer us, for a couple of coins, synesthesia via voyages in submarines, space ships or time tunnels?

Enthusiasm as much as unease are possible reactions to so uncertain and mobile a picture as that of the disarticulated underclasses of Latin American societies. Even in pessimism one may encounter a certain dose of pleasure, insofar as exercising renunciation can supply a liberating effect for the one practicing it. On the other hand, optimism likewise can be a subproduct of pessimism: facing the loss of utopias, one renounces that critical action that commits itself to change. Attention is displaced towards the small pleasures that a world in decomposition can offer. The optimist is, to some extent, a transfigured pessimist, capable of "reading" reality with an ingenious mixture of candor and acuity, thus avoiding the heavy weight of pending integration, the guilt caused by the system's injustices, and concern with the exclusions emanating from the styles of development current in Latin America. Proof of the vastness of the changes required to escape from these problems is that they require almost limitless power and they dead-end in conflict. From this proof, one decides—quickly forgetting that a decision is involved—to concentrate on the immediate: one's body, one's peers, one's current project.

Nevertheless, the question remains open: From what place to center life's joy in this discontinuous, uncertain, fragmented, shifting scenario? Some conjectures follow.

Life's joy lies in turning change into ecstasy. On whatever scale, in whatever media, everything changes with growing acceleration. Technological impact, ecstasies of communication, the globalization of markets and social deterioration are some factors responsible for this acceleration. Facing this, two possibilities: either die of vertigo, or enjoy vertigo. It would be necessary to develop the second of the two possibilities, to learn how to enjoy the ceaseless recompositions of the backdrop, to delight in the cadence of change. Nonetheless, the urgent is still pending: is it possible to enjoy the vertigo of the excluded?

Life's joy lies in the lightness of ties. There's no firm tie to the future, today's job, the present moment's interlocutors. Everything can be changed tomorrow and we'll find ourselves in another, uncalculated moment, in another job and in close communication with new people. Facing this, two possibilities: either die of living a provisional existence, or immerse oneself in it. The second requires extraordinary plasticity, not only to resituate oneself in this sequence of provisional ties, but to be able to identify oneself with them while they last.

Life's joy lies in occupying the interstitial areas, the areas in-between. Facing a reality which is simultaneously fragmented and enormously resistant to structural changes, one can substitute the reconciliatory, liberatory joy promised by revolution with enthusiasm for little utopias or gaps within a disenchanted world. This enthusiasm can spur one to lead an initiative of communal participation; to identify oneself with the ephemeral and circumstantial symbols used by those who reject the status quo, the Establishment; to come and go between new social movements that are born and die; to sporadically transgress a social norm; to ridicule power in complicity with some peers; or to capitalize, taking advantage of the gaps that macroeconomic disequilibrium creates. All this can be a source of rejoicing, however briefly.

Life's joy lies in rescuing from romanticism the bet on passion. Lacking redemption through revolution or integration, there remains the possibility of a passion that temporarily inhabits the field of fantasy that carries the body to an almost mystic reverberation. In this sense, a resurgence of romanticism shouldn't be surprising.

Finally, life's joy can come from taking pleasure in forms. Diversity brings with it a proliferation of images and sensations. If the culture of revolution — and integration — subordinates form to content and means

to ends, this subordination is not evident in the culture of disenchantment. The skin becomes a second form of consciousness, and from the
skin it is possible to contemplate the environment cinematographically,
since the environment is displaced and modified according to a rhythm
closer to cinema than to old-fashioned reality. The primacy of the substantial gives way to the contemplation of the diverse.

Once again, the question lies in wait: Do these motives of joy—seduction by vertigo, the lightness of ties, the interstitial adventure, the adventure of in-between places, the bet on individual passion, the exaltation of
forms, and the consequent loss of substantiality—favor social, national,
Latin American integration? Is integration conceivable from vertigo, lightness, the in-between, passion, the aesthetic? Or, on the contrary, is there no
more solid directionality, no firmer connection required?

Provisional or uncertain, disenchanted or integrated, the moods of
Latin America are not clear. Perhaps the revolution is, after all, a concept
that endures, although orphaned of an image capable of fleshing it out, in
the collective consciousness. Perhaps the integration of the peoples—
among themselves and with others—is a still-pending task that will have
to be taken up again, after this poor Sunday that we are living. In the
meantime, I believe that the commentaries spilled out here speak of a
certain cultural tempering, operating at large, in the air.

Unless my subjectivity, dear reader, has nothing to do with yours.

Notes

1   During the sixties, the seventies, and the beginning of the eighties, the political culture
of the left fostered the notion of revolution within which personal existence was meaningful insofar as it was fully consecrated to the radical change of the social order. From a
strong project with a substantial utopian content, individual life appeared redeemed
and charged through with meaning. Today, with the so-called end of utopias and
strong ideologies, the personal life of many has to seek other channels to "justify itself"
or to give it sense. Thus the "necessity of giving new meaning to personal existence," no
longer by way of maximalist discourse or projects, but in a postmodern climate in
which the grand narratives have been weakened, and in which meaning is more closely
linked to the day-to-day, to the molecular, to the human scale.

2   The idea of "integration" appears and circulates throughout development discourse in
Latin America in the years following WWII. "Integration" refers to processes in which
different social groups move progressively closer to participating in the dynamics and
benefits of progress and of modernization. In this way, integration has been systematically understood as occurring at the nexus of various discrete phenomena. These phe-

nomena include: progressive participation in the economically active population, in modern, active employment positions that are increasingly productive and at higher salaries; access to higher education and thus to greater possibilities of future socio-economic mobility; expanding consumer power, which implies access to a growing and diversified range of goods and services; improved housing, that is, access to housing of a higher quality that is more connected to the modern infrastructure; institutionalized access to health services and social security. The opposition between "the integrated" and "the excluded" has been understood, in Latin America, in relation to realizing, or not realizing, these goals. Closely tied to the idea of social mobility and of adjustment to norms, the concept of integration only recently incorporates new aspects such as the cultural affirmation of ethnic minorities, the variable of gender and the strengthening of social capital.

3 In the first place, the precarious is always provisional, but not vice versa. The best way to define the precarious is "with high social vulnerability," that is, alluding to social groups that lack social security and have low educational levels, unstable or persistent unemployment, and weak social networks. The provisional best refers to the "new style" of those who are integrated into the hyped-up rhythm of globalization. They are not committed to long term projects, they easily change direction in their economic activities, they are relatively secularized in their daily life — and as such, their values are more ad hoc.

2 ✳ Disenchanted and Triumphant Toward the 21st Century: A Prospect of Cultural Moods in South America

Bewildering Politics

In the beginning of 1989, who could have foreseen that the rise of fuel prices in Venezuela would trigger a descent of the excluded from the hills to Caracas, with Carlos Andrés Pérez's return to power bringing the first popular response, sketched across the skin of the continent's most schizoid capital: the taboo image of a city sacked by its excluded members?

Who would have imagined that in Ecuador, in June of 1990, under the governing image of the highly literate, much praised, stuffy Borja, indigenous peoples from the mountains all over the country would emerge, like furtive phantoms, to paralyze the highways and settle accounts according to their own vernacular customs?

Who would have thought that a silent, oriental figure with no political experience, would become, over the course of an evening, the president that Peruvians would choose, through a popular vote, to show them the way out of the quagmire?

Everything's explicable, once the deeds are done. But the surprises of politics in South America share a common characteristic: from indigenous revolts to the eruptions of popular movements in the precarious peace of the cities, to the named and unforeseeable preferences of the electorate, social energies are difficult to rationalize. The collective imaginary is populated by passions, desires, and images that exceed the political calculus, inundating it with surprises. No one fails to recognize that South American societies have been normalizing in very heterogeneous ways, in their productive structure as in their symbolic order. If something distinguishes them, it's precisely this mixture: culture whisks together the ingredients of secularization and normalization in the strangest ways.

Despite everything, South American modernization has undeniably acquired renewed impetus. No one can pull together the force and will sufficient to contain, revert, or undermine it. A new secularizing crusade imposes a code of universalistic pretensions. Its gaudiest manifestations are an updated, instrumental rationality, accelerated privatization, the opening of markets, and a race against time to modernize what can be modernized and to administrate what can't be modernized. Yet the libretto repeatedly falls apart, for it's undeniable that this sham secularization lands in the airports, businesses, and masses of the South American continent, who elect as their governors beatific administrators such as Fujimori, television technocrats like Collor de Melo, Hollywood patriots like Menem. The devout and the bandits are incorporated into the dynamic of transnationalized markets without ceasing to be devout or bandits. The sacked city or blockaded mountains are gestures of the same masses. The returns to democracy in the Southern Cone begin in fiesta and continue in litany. And the more this secular modernization extends, the more churches of every sort proliferate.

That all this has been said before doesn't make it less true. For reasons different from those of development-based modernization, open market modernization fractures on the side of culture. We must situate ourselves within that fracture in the course of the following pages, trying to compose a map where the disenchanted and the triumphant fill our countries with new cultural signs. From within this fracture we will ultimately attempt to bring together, as much as possible, the art of sleight of hand and the science of anticipating the future.

*From the Side of the Disenchanted: Where Are
the Desires for Emancipation Headed?*

The death of the image of a possible revolution struck at the militants of
the left, critical intellectuals, and a nucleus of politically conscious workers. It erased from the future, even in its diffuse range of hope, the image
of social change as capable of bringing about liberation from poverty and
alienation. This erasure is a form of death and cultural transfiguration
in society.

In South America, no country exists that has not, in its moment, internalized this image of the possible future. Its incorporation not only transformed the forms and limits of political discourse, but also intermingled
with the "dance of symbols" afloat in heterogenous South American societies. Popular culture's syncretic assimilation of the left's proposals probably — and contradictorily — originated in what Marx called the opium of
the people: popular religiosity. There, famished for content, were the
eschatological feelings, messianic and geared towards redemption, of a
people with a Christian soul. While highly literate social critics could feel
the promise of the socialist revolution as an historic necessity, the people
took that promise as the concrete hope of liberation.[1] Redemption by way
of Massive Social Change, the end of hard times, and the advent of the
Kingdom of the Poor thus came to form part of the popular imagination.

To enter into the set of causes that finished off this "concrete utopia" is
now beside the point. Military coups, the boom of neoliberal ideology,
real socialism's collapse, the rationalization of the market, and the prag-
matist's triumph in the political arena are all visible signs draining both
the hope and historical necessity of revolution. At one extreme, neoliberalism appropriated the word "revolution," stuffing it with the euphoria of
worldwide capitalism in the making.[2] The questions, then, are as follows:
What's presently happening with the mass of cultural energy that flowed
towards the bet on a socialist liberation, and where does this mass of
energy seem aimed in the future?

A suggestive hypothesis is that the withdrawal of physical and discursive forces of socialist liberation has provoked a deployment of diverse
spaces for variously reinserting the energies mentioned above. These
spaces promote the accelerated expansion of popular religious currents in
which individual liberation is quite independent of collective change, and
the diffuse presence of Christian base organizations that seek liberation in
the neighborhood's everyday life. The fragments of a theory of the revolu-

tion metamorphose into reasons for a theology of liberation. Aren't these the ways in which the "liberatory-redemptive drive" is exercised nowadays as partial relays of a possible revolution? And how much of the epic energy of the socialist revolution is conserved in these interstices?

Other, less beatific, exits are in use. Cynical hedonism overlooks the vacant screen, marginal hedonism cracks it. The scenario formally occupied by the emancipation of the masses is now populated by the restless signs of esotericism, for now there are no longer any masses. Yet it assuredly guarantees that personal life will be filled with a new richness of meaning, a near obesity of meanings. The Tarot, the *I Ching,* orientalist currents, Zen or Nostradamus return us to the exercise of permanent interpretation and the tranquility of having an imminent catharsis. But again: without masses. On the other extreme, a guerrilla force became, during the 1980s, more and more impermeable, syncretic, eschatological, and, paradoxically, even more lacking of a future.

There's more on the map of the revolution's orphans: a revival of the popular communitarian spirit in which former leftist militants, converted to a secularized discourse of the culture of solidarity, coexist with small base organizations that recognize this discourse as their own and involuntarily reappear within it as new redeeming agents for social change. Within these same neighborhoods lives a more explosive drive, a new form of urban revolt (announced in Santiago de Chile in 1983–84 and in Caracas in 1989) where accumulated discontent motivates looting. Under the image of a looted city, the fire of apocalypse bursts into flame. Frustration and everyday humiliation may be the motives, yet the scenic effect suggests a bit more: the work of a spirit wreaking justice, unleashing its menacing lightning bolts on supermarkets and other symbols of exclusionary modernization.

This surely isn't all, nor is it all so well defined. But exaggeration helps illustrate the idea that secularization in the South American continent didn't make a blank slate of the popular imagination. The promise of socialist revolution (like other programs for mass emancipation, proposed by leftist Enlightenment as one more secularizing step, perhaps the most ambitious step of all) channeled a torrent of energy that wasn't totally secularized. One might confuse, but not deny the syncretisms involved in this synthesis of the future with the past. The interstices in which this torrent of energy presently relocates itself, maintaining the vitality of its hopes and its flows, aren't very clear either. The preceding description hints at contradictory de-secularizing pressures moving underneath the triumphalist display of market ideology as the last relay of the race towards a secularization with universalist pretensions.

Whether housed in a church building or not, today almost all churches acquire or open up spaces for communion. The very space of culture, understood as a space in which values are created, recreated, and used, loses its so-called homogeneity. This fissure could be an antidote to the secularizing crusade of world capitalism, but at the same time it shunts all "alternative" spaces into the category of the interstitial.[3] De-centering has its luminous side in the installation of diversity, and its impotent side in the fragmentation of collective dreams. And the more porous the society, the more disparate and diverse the promise of emancipation. The empty pigeonhole of social revolution need no more than fall apart into fragments, in order to return to fill up again.[4]

This de-centering accelerates with the new impetus of the culture industry. Global communication and increasingly diversified access to new cultural goods dissolve the limits. Many believe that in this new cultural consumption they can encounter a new figure for the utopia of diversity. The illusion of a subject-producer-of-the-world can be rediscovered in the new interactive forms of the culture industry, where each receptor of messages easily moves on to emit them. The ideal of autonomy becomes associated with the facility for loading goods and services tied to one's own personal menu within the cultural industry. But once again, the dubious impact on societies with low levels of social integration is unknown. The unresolved division between those who are modern and those who are not is exacerbated by the gap between those who are computerized and those who are not. The segmentation between the modern and the traditional is defined less by the topics consumed (for the limits between low and high culture are erased) than by the level of "performance" in each sector.

The corollary of the previous treatises is that with regard to a future in which the fleshed-out image of social revolution has lost verisimilitude, emancipatory energies are reabsorbed by new capitalist modernization. Or their current is redirected, as a pendulum, towards segmented and transfigured forms of de-secularization, or they look to channel a new ideal of cultural diversity through new forms of symbolic consumption (especially in the segmented connection with the cultural-industrial complex). Some of the contents of that new ideal or those new forms turn explicitly religious. Other, more apparently secular ones likewise resist the exclusionist secularization consecrated as status quo, whether for the present or as a new historical necessity for the future. It is from this type of secularization, which constitutes the central point of the next topic, that the new triumphant culture is made.

On the Side of the Triumphant: Booming Culture at the Crossroads of the Market and Instrumental Rationality

Capitalism occupies the prophecy that Marx served for socialism: to realize its utopia, it becomes world capitalism. The opening of markets is imposed, in rapid steps, all over the world. South America revises its comparative advantages and response to the stabilizing regulations dictated from the North. With the political spectrum, the displacement towards what is euphemistically termed the center at once hides and reveals this option: accepting the rules of the game of transnationalized markets requires forgetting redistributive reforms of a structural character and using pragmatic rationality to guarantee the democratic order and safeguard its institutions. The adjustment programs don't especially vary from candidate to candidate, or from country to the country. It's clear, however, that the pact's instruments vary, as do the reforms of legislative power, the formulas of administrative decentralization, and the rhythms of political and economic opening.

Two cultural phenomena underlie this shared symptomology. On the one hand, technological innovation has accelerated exponentially, and the expansive rhythm of instrumental rationality has penetrated multiple spheres, from the most public to the most private spheres of human life. On the other hand, the institution of a market without borders as the axis of social integration exacerbates use relations. The zeal for lucre no longer goes against the current of social cohesion, of ideology converted into system. On the contrary, it returns as the virtuous individual motivation for competition between businesses, not just in classical texts of political economy, but in everyday life.

These characteristics aren't new. Their critics have exhaustively denounced them. But the new worldwide hegemony of the market and the new differentiating powers of technology can exacerbate them to unprecedented degrees. The "dominant mode of secularization" is seated, today, on two axes: exhaustive use of technology and privatization. It's pertinent, then, to break them down, by means of analysis.

The culture of instrumentalization

Instrumental rationality penetrates in very uneven ways, in South America. Just compare the computing infrastructure in elite schools with its absolute absence from public education. In the former, the student mentality is increasingly oriented to a logic of achievement, which would be a productive rationalization of education on the South American scale. Meanwhile the public schools remain entrenched in an anachronistic, third-rate encyclopedism.

In the sphere of work, the logic of achievement is like an invisible hand underlying the growing differentiation of productive processes. The starkest expression of this logic appears in the maxim of competitiveness: be more productive or leave the market. While it's certainly true that South American business culture spuriously incorporates this rationality, its midrange perspectives seem conditioned by the imperative of efficiency above all. If "easy money" was the upper classes' parasite formula during the boom of financial capitalism,[5] the 1990s insinuated a turn away from "easy money": either businesses augment their productive-competitive capacity in real markets, or no amount of speculation will save them. The magic word, efficiency, figures not just in courses for business executives. Mass media and political discourse also conform to the logic of efficiency.

I am not trying to deny the importance of productivity for development, particularly in societies such as ours that have not managed to forge a business culture capable of putting itself above the temptations of "*rentismo*," living from one's investment income. What's disquieting, in the mid-range, is the conditioning of the value assigned to productivity in the symbolic order. In what measure will the value assigned to productivity be capable of absorbing the ties of solidarity between (and within) social groups?

In industrialized countries, this new secularization has been absorbed as the promise of greater individual development. Insofar as the individual's relation to his or her surroundings is increasingly mediated through operations of "efficient use" of information, the possibilities of individual development are expanded, rather than leveled. Instrumental reason seems not to inhibit the differentiation of identities, but rather to constitute a cultural heritage capable of putting itself at the service of personality development. This is, at the least, a defense of pro-technological discourse. To each of us according to our specializations, and from each of us according to our motivations. Almost like a game. The culture of software permits the translation of instrumental reason into personal passion. Individualism and the progressive use of technology in private and public lives become compatible in time, at least, as a possible utopia.

South America insinuates a scenario where other contradictions render this reconciliation less thinkable. In Brazil, the country central to the continent's industrialization, the promises of technological individualism will be fleshed out, with luck, among the third of the population that has been modernized, by leaps and bounds. Among the other two thirds, lower levels of income and minimal access to modernity's benefits constitute an impenetrable wall against which the expectations for personal differentiation shatter into a thousand pieces. Even as Brazil produces computers and exports nuclear technology and cultural industry, in the country's rural Northeast the population's life expectancy is sixteen years below that of the population in the South. In all the countries of South America, the requirements for bringing about a macroeconomic equilibrium and to modernize what can be modernized, added to tremendous historic, productive, and social heterogeneity, impose a giant question mark on the happy confluence of individual development with the increased use of technology. In an economy overflowing with contingents of the excluded, where the mediations between their collective organization and public power are fragile, the logic of efficiency increasingly penetrates all spheres of life, thus increasing the potential for the manipulation of the excluded by the integrated. Societies as inequitable as ours can increase the use of technology. Even as such high levels of exclusion remain, the increasingly modernized management of poverty will be one of the most fertile fields for technological modernization, responding as much to the technology owner's zeal for lucre as to the operator's instrumental rationality.

Another phenomenon makes this diffusion of technical rationality more problematic. In the culture industry, the modern is no longer defined by a hierarchy of cultural genres or by the size of factories, but by the incorporation of impalpable technology in the production of messages. For example, a canned TV program is more modern than a cultural program, if the former manages to integrate itself into international programming and the latter only appears locally, with low ratings. Or the inverse: a cultural program is more modern than a soap opera if it has introduced more counterpoints, a greater variety of discursive planes and iconic combinations, better optical definition, and/or a more dynamic thematic treatment. In other words, the most recent effects of communicational global-ization and technological diversification in cultural-industrial complexes mean that the idea of modern culture is linked not to modern contents but to the capitalization of technological supplies (which include production and a sense of opportunity). The modern is defined more by performance than by content, more by technological packaging than by message, more by the rhythm of innovation than by the product's specificity.

This mutation carves its new signs in the cultural imagination. Editing becomes more important than the plot, effect more sought after than substance. The *mestizaje* (intermixing) of cultures is subordinated to dra-matic logic on the monitor, and the recognition of diversity increasingly resembles a "chronomatic mercantile" optimization for circulating infor-mation. The new industrial-cultural complex subordinates cultural diver-sity and identities to the logic of Disney.

The vision summarized in the preceding paragraphs doubtless smacks of Manichean tendencies. The divide between integrated and excluded isn't so clear-cut. Technological expansion can also come, in lesser degrees, to the less productive population. It's worth noting, however, that the previous paragraph exaggerates for the purpose of illustration. As an effect (though not a guarantee) of the deployment of instrumental reason and technological expansion, individual development is conceivable only to the extent that social integration in South American societies makes it viable. Yet, the effects of this deployment tend to the reverse — to intersub-jective manipulation, consecrating relations of use and command within a highly inequitable social order.

The culture of privatization

A phantom circles the globe: privatization. To list its causes and motives is to reiterate what has been said above: inefficiency of the public sector, entropy of the State as benefactor and businessman, capitalism's ideologi-cal and productive hegemony, and/or legitimate demands for greater au-tonomy among social actors. But what have been the impacts of this privatizing wave on culture in South America? In what senses are people's lives and values modified?

The internalization of culture that accompanies privatization can't im-pact distinct social segments in a homogeneous manner. In the modern business sectors, privatization is likely accompanied by an intensified feel-ing of being in the limelight of national life. This, too, is reflected in the current proposals for development, where private agents from the business sector occupy the best seats. The desire to expand the business sector seems revitalized by an apparently limitless field of private action. Within that field, the diversification of activities and inversions multiplies the network of peer relations. These relations can be provisional and "tactical" in a world where the leading actors are themselves defined as fields of continual change. The feeling of opportunity becomes more acute than ever. The flow of capital accelerates and the eye should keep a close watch on these sleight-of-hand games. Rapid and lucid decisions make for a good, modern businessperson.

Within the field of consumption, the upper classes internalize the same pattern of diversification and acceleration. With redoubled speed, the globalization of national economies spurs the imitation of consumer norms among potential peers from the industrialized world. In order to capitalize on the offer of a growing range of goods and services, the upper sectors have to maintain the same hyperkinetic activity of consumption and investment. All of life is rationalized in order to fill the everyday with multiple special effects: tennis tournaments, courses on stress reduction, gyms with sophisticated technology, the production of home videos, computer games, communication with international networks from a terminal at home, group tours, and the immortal television.

The feelings of prominence and of provisionality coexist in the new spirit of the booming classes. In a dissolving movement, privatization individualizes yet submerges the links between prominence and provisionality. The market's density lightens ties. Private life is divided into many lives, with distinct reference groups, united by the slender thread of complicities. The word "superficial" is disguised with the maxim, "up to date."

The proposed description doubtless smacks of caricature. But, once again: the exaggeration helps illustrate, by contrast, the temper of the times.

Among the poor, the privatizing wave is internalized with very distinct effects. The Welfare State fades away, as do some consecrated mechanisms of social mobility, whether effective or symbolic. This fading away generates contradictory tendencies in the orbit of the excluded. The culture of survival is expressed in the solidarity of the barrio and in the jungle of anomie. Uncertainty with respect to the future has more to do with fear than with creativity, yet the need to vanquish fear fosters creativity. The private is necessarily far more public among the poor than in the upper sectors: the street is the place for resolving the most pressing needs, and for attacking or joining one's neighbors. Here, the provisional changes its name and becomes simply, fully uncertain. Lightness becomes orphanhood; diversification becomes fragmentation.

What happens to sensitivity? With the culture of poverty exacerbated as "the culture of restricted reproduction," disenchanted introversion, aggressive extroversion and spasmodic communitarianism all follow. Privatization simultaneously creates an obligation to action and a condemnation to subsistence. At one extreme, in the widening gap between expectations and achievements, self confidence is fractured; reality becomes more unreal. Democracy is converted, for a period of time, into the symbolic substitute for social mobility. It can exercise social identity by way of political participation, communitarian initiative, television connections, and freedom of expression. But without social mobility or prospects for gaining access to acceptable levels of well being, democracy itself demotivates the poor. The private becomes privation.

Situations of massive exclusion also generate a massive frustration of expectations. What happens to the historical promise of development that for various decades looked to dynamize and integrate the peoples of Latin America? The longer it's postponed, the more the frustration grows among those who are perpetually postponed. Our region of the world is distinguished by the special discontinuity of its material progress and by its scarce capacity for relatively equitable distribution. Time exacerbates rather than mitigates the differences, widening the gap between expectations and achievement. The discourse of development makes promises and promotes aspirations which are internalized without creating access to mobility and consumption. This is particularly acute in the masses of young people who suffer the worst combination. They experience greater difficulties with regard to joining the labor market in a job position corresponding to their level of education; a prior process of education in which the economic value of their own formation has been injected and subsequently denied by the lack of opportunities for work; and great identification, by way of cultural consumption, with new and varied goods and services to which the great masses of young people cannot gain access, even as these goods and services constitute symbols of social mobility.

We confront, then, a paradoxical inversion of signs. There is asynchrony between increased difficulty and discontinuity in the processes of socioeconomic integration. (That difficulty is now associated with crisis, adjustment, and economic conversion.) There is furthermore a tendency towards intensified integration on the symbolic-cultural level (which is an effect of a political openness occurring primarily by way of cultural and communicative consumption). Thus synchrony and intensified integration could, over the next few years, constitute a significant change in development's meaning and discourse, in our continent.

The scarcity of food in impoverished households coexists with the obesity of messages consumed on television. This abundant impoverishment among the poor contrasts with the provisional quality of the always "in good shape" condition of those who benefit from the new pattern of growth.

Again I exaggerate or generalize. And again, the dramatization helps to illustrate the feeling of the times in which we live. Surely the cultural trauma of the continent isn't exhausted by the two extremes on the social scale. Rather, these extremes suggest the limits of the discourse universe. The terror of uncertainty and the temptation to diversify operate as two great cultural phantoms, situated in the antipodes of a horizon of reference that permits individuals and collective actors to formulate their own mediations.

Playing with Prospects

Referring to the contradictory features stressed in the preceding pages, what cultural mutations await us now that South America has crossed the year 2000? The following hypotheses are useful for letting the imagination run loose.

Privatizing secularization, clothed in transnational, technologizing rationality, brings all kinds of fundamentalisms in its wake.

The new secularizing impulse that comes with the greater diffusion of technical rationality, mass media's explosive impact, the globalization of markets, and the defeat of socialism as the last total utopia in western politics all provoke defensive and fundamentalist reactions in many sectors. These reactions vary from one region to the next. The case of Islam, for example, not only illustrates how religious fundamentalism impacts economic and political relations, but also, inversely, how the lack of social integration (involving the modernizing and secularizing dynamic) reinforces cultural integration (by way of messianic traditionalism). In India, the emergence of the Hinduist movement only partially rejects the universalist aspects of modernization. Instead, it proposes to constitute an alternative, replacing the secular, pluralist tradition of the Congress Party. In the former Yugoslavia, and in the formerly Soviet Caucasus and in Russia, antimodern cultural identities acquire greater impetus in the face of the dissolution of statist and centralist secularization. These identities oscillate between irrational nationalisms and new forms of religious messianism. In the South American scene, Shining Path in Peru was an extreme case of how an end-of-the-millennium discourse, mixed with Andean myths and pro-Chinese communism, channels social frustration by way of a stark violence. Across this diversity, there nonetheless exists a marked tendency to global-scale dissipation of the ideological war between capitalism and socialism, and to the reinforcement of the secularizing wave by way of markets and the barrage of mass media. This causes forms of "anti-secular entrenchment" to flower, founded less on political-ideological discourse than on closed cultures. The Persian Gulf War, the conflicts in Bosnia-Herzegovina, the Armenian-Azerbaijanian dispute, the enmity between Pakistan and India: all these are clashes between entrenched cultural identities.

In the case of our continent the increasing impact of Catholic fundamentalism can be observed and is exhibited in various countries, among the middle and upper sectors, channeled, above all, by Opus Dei. This fundamentalism doesn't oppose the privatizing and mercantilizing wave, although it does oppose the liberality of customs that said secularization provokes. Reaction to the menace of the "death of God" is an effect of capitalist secularization that tends to be charged with moral traditionalism, without being any less pro-capitalist. The more marked the effect of secularization, the greater the possibilities of cultural rootedness that fundamentalism will have in reaction to that secularization.

Motivating this traditionalist reaction is the dissolving impact of various processes, including the deregulation of economic life (with its effects of social fragmentation) and the expansion of a technological rationality that depletes the present of transcendental values and the future of ultimate ends, thus reinforcing the provisional nature of social ties (effected by a kind of cost-benefit rationality that sooner or later will begin to undermine even family ties). Facing anomie in sectors marginalized by development, and the softening of customs in the sectors integrated into the new modernity, the expansion of Catholic and Protestant fundamentalism will be the dominant receptacle for mitigating these deaths of God, not just because of fundamentalism's historical presence in South America, but also because of the power it presently wields through its social networks, its power in the means of mass communication, its financial resources, and its pressures on key points in the state apparatus.

The consequences of this rise of Catholic fundamentalism in the field of culture could provoke acute contradictions between tradition and liberality. Young people on the continent could radicalize towards these two extremes. Ascetic isolationism and frantic hedonism could form the cultural prototypes in a new scenario of confrontations, above all, among young people. Catholic fundamentalism isn't the only kind of fundamentalism with the propensity for expansion over the coming years, although it could well be the one with the greatest power and cultural influence. Countries with high degrees of disintegration could also see violent messianic movements from the left. These movements will probably be marginal, with no prospects for altering the pattern of capitalist development, yet they would disrupt the public order and the security of citizens. Shining Path has been the extreme example. The validity of the continent's democracies will probably guarantee that these movements don't reach the magnitude or disruptive capacity of Shining Path. The option for a fundamentalism of armed leftists could nonetheless constitute a means for channeling the accumulated discontent and the lack of utopias supplied in political discourse.

A first motive for violent messianic movements from the left would consist of belonging to a group with an accentuated degree of collective identification. Facing social exclusion and democracy's lack of material responses over a sustained period of time, organic belonging to an insurrectionary movement could serve as a strategy of social identification. A second motive would be the adoption of a world outlook reconciled to a personal life project. Unreserved identification with an eschatological utopia can work as a form of inclusion within exclusion. Facing hopelessness and a lack of referents for collective identification, insurgency rises in the margins: the margins of society, of law, of democracy. The same messianic and redemptory sediments scattered when the images of mass emancipation toppled. Those scattered sediments, added to the persistent structural conditions of social exclusion, could provide a breeding ground for these kinds of dispersed groups.

Another fundamentalism that could spring to life would be one with indigenous content, rooted in Andean countries. Its forces are probably based in the Andean countries with the greatest degree of ethnic segregation: Peru, and to a lesser degree, Ecuador and Bolivia. In these countries there exists a cultural and ideological tradition that could provide a foothold for indigenist fundamentalism. Facing a pattern of secularization with exclusionary social effects, this tradition could be radicalized, unearthing the historical memory of pre-Hispanic or anti-Hispanic Andean utopias. Indigenist fundamentalism's expansion could lead to a cultural reaction against both secularization and modernization, located at the farthest remove from Catholic fundamentalism, but with an analogous fastening to tradition. Marginalized urban populations, esoteric groups, and disenchanted intellectuals could adhere to the indigenist vanguard. Antimodern and antiwestern cultural entrenchment could result in a highly confrontational scenario in the field of culture, and a disruptive effect on the political order.

A final fundamentalism could be anchored in the very heart of secularization: instrumental-capitalist rationality. New technocracies will champion the technological utopia, the redemptive goodwill of the market, and the providential triumph of administrative logic. Back in modernity's origins, Francis Bacon imagined such a technological utopia, which he named The New Atlantis, but its totalitarian bias led subsequent individualism and liberalism to consign it to oblivion. The present euphoria of capitalism's apologists could reconcile technological and liberal utopias. It's no accident that Francis Fukujama's fragile essay, entitled *The End of History*, found such widespread acceptance, resonating through the liberalizing right wing of academia and politics.

The triumphalist proclamation of capitalism as the world order, and the uncritical optimism that exalts the virtuous impacts of technology, are anchored in the modern business sector, in the well remunerated public technocracies, in the networks of consultants to booming business and in the many intellectuals who've been orphaned of *grand-récits*. This uncritical triumphalism announces the end of ideologies and of utopias even as it tries to construct itself as the only ideology and utopia. Its fundamentalist drift could be due its own need for self-ratification in facing other more cautious (or more critical) interlocutors. Or it could be a cultural strategy for consolidating its hegemony. While the exhaustive globalization of the capitalist order and of instrumental rationality appear as historically necessary (at least in the consciousness of its new apologists), the tendency towards a liberal-technocratic fundamentalism could become reality. In a new, modern, and pacific crusade, the death of God would be deified at last.

Lacking utopias of popular emancipation, lacking stable channels
for social mobility, the violence of the excluded could unleash a culture of death.

The loss of normative referents among the excluded, an effect of the fading of stable channels for social mobility and shared hopes for mass emancipation, will foment fragmented forms of "inverted" socialization. These could be expressed through the proliferation of marginal subcultures that turn on self-affirmation by way of violence.

The lack of emancipatory utopias furthermore coincides with an historical inflection: discontinuous development and the resultant lack of social integration widen the gap in expectations. Contributing to this gap are unjust distribution of the fruits of growth, the greater regressive impact of crisis and adjustments on the wages of low- and middle-wage workers, and permanent visual contact with goods displayed by the television screen. Among the excluded sectors there is a growing feeling that those who benefit from this distributive injustice of goods enjoy a certain socioeconomic impunity, just as the wealthier sectors or the dominant political forces can come to enjoy impunity in their abuse of subordinated groups. Because of the lack of distributive justice in development, the lack of penal justice with regard to abuse and discriminations, and of emancipatory utopias to channel this massive discontent, it's quite likely that the response from the marginalized will open across a range of reactive violence.

Criminal violence in the cities offers the most visible case of marginal subculture. Within a logic of reciprocity, criminal violence offers the excluded a way of processing their exclusion. Facing a juridical, cultural, and socioeconomic system of laws that excludes them, criminal delinquents affirm a legality of their own in which they see themselves simultaneously as protagonists and beneficiaries. By way of their action they construct an order in which the violated and abused is the other, the possible victim. In this way the relation of exclusions is both inverted and preserved: the delinquent is integrated into a community of peers in which mechanisms of mutual recognition, shared slang, and "active disenchantment" all exist. Delinquent violence thus manifests the implicit violence of structural exclusion, violating those same exclusionary structures.

The expansion in the traffic and consumption of drugs among poor sectors will function as an unprecedented multiplier within this subculture. Especially among the young, access to barbiturates and cocaine derivatives will exercise an annihilating effect on minimal norms of sociability. The same lack of prospects for social integration or occupational mobility constitute the detonator. Under the effects of drugs and alcohol, the subjects experience a symbolic compensation in which they recover, in a substitute and counterproductive way, part of their lost self-esteem. Among television actors or high-ranking executives, the drug subculture has very different connotations than among the popular sectors. In the latter, it nourishes the subculture of delinquency, aggravated by the kind of crimes that an addict commits, which are always disproportionate to the booty: a murder for a modest sum, sufficient for that night's fix. Most addictive drugs bring their victims to total devaluation of the other, constituting a rapid road into delinquency and the loss of basic norms of respect for the rest, effects which cities such as Lima, Medellín, Bogotá or Rio de Janeiro are already beginning to feel. Drug cartels may have produced a way of life in Colombia among young people from the age of thirteen hiring themselves out as murderers, but the proliferation of such murder-for-hire belongs to a subculture of crime where patronage also mitigates exclusion.

The risks of the upcoming years aren't only the increased volume of delinquents but also the absolute devaluation of their potential victims' lives. Widening drug rings and the murderer's "normalization" could likewise extend into other circles of marginality. This deviant symptom is the underside of a triumphant culture's exaltation of the market and technology, both of which reinforce social gaps. The triumphalism of the integrated will have to confront this deviant answer among the excluded.

This will have alarming effects. The culture of death, overflowing the margins of South American societies — no longer as State terror, but the absence of the State — spills into the city centers and rich neighborhoods. Self-affirmation through negating the other (including the life of the other) will be the starkest, most fearsome shape that instrumental rationality will assume, among all of its exclusivizing effects. The constant threat to personal, bodily integrity won't be a problem just in Rio de Janeiro or Caracas. The drama of citizens' insecurity will be extended towards traditionally peaceable cities — as is now happening in Buenos Aires or Santiago de Chile — and it will give a very concrete foundation to the general paranoia. Its consequence would be a spiraling rise in everyday aggression. People's dwellings will take on the appearance of fortresses. Life in open spaces will be seen as restricted by an increasingly complex network of provisions and precautions. The private will become increasingly hermetic and the public, increasingly policed. Death by way of physical aggression will circle like a phantom in people's dreams. The reaction from below, to a violence that is institutionalized, or implicit in the unjust distribution of wealth will be superseded by a new pitiless counterreaction from above. Public or private policies will enter into a logic of death, most chillingly expressed in the massacre of street children in Rio de Janeiro, in a species of preventive rationality that deprives life of value: street children are murdered in order "to reduce future delinquency." The logic of death here unites with a dehumanizing form of instrumental reason.

This hypothesis smacks of apocalyptic thinking. It's certainly possible that democracy in the continent will open channels of political and symbolic integration for the masses of excluded young people, preventing the consecration of violence in the form of constituted, extended subcultures. But recent years show us a progressive tendency towards criminal violence. Extrapolated towards the future, it becomes alarming.

Diversification with fragmentation (of spheres of competency, of collective participation, and of consumption) will be the most important cultural effects of secularizing modernization.

This might be the scenario of postmodernity in South America. Once the images of the emancipation of the masses, the totalizing utopias and the norms of a unitary culture are diluted, then the secularizing effects of the market and instrumental rationality might effect the dispersion of social life. Ties will become provisional and precarious, with each person following his or her own personal life project and tastes. The expansion of a professionalized culture market might open segmented options, within which a wide variety of micro-societies could be constituted.

Within this context of producers and consumers in the culture industry, the mass displacement of professionalism is evident when we observe how in industrialized countries millions of children operate computers with an ease that once (not long ago) seemed reserved to engineers and those on the cutting edge of technology. As apprenticeships become quick and diverse, little training is required to move from neophyte to initiate. The diffusion of these new cultural practices might permit a positive expansion of the forms of symbolic belonging and of cultural self-affirmation. De-centering the emission of messages in the culture industry might even democratize symbolic consumption in the region.

This would be countered by a tendency to introversion in the poor sectors, whose communitarian networks would change into parallel societies where the culture of survival would barely touch the State, spaces of greater public visibility, and other social groups. Participation in the cultural-industrial complex would appear to be restricted by the lack of access to the new knowledge and know-how that allows active linkages with the new forms of cultural consumption.

Indifference towards other groups would be countered by provisional but strong cohesion with the peer group. Some tactical alliances of an instrumental sort could serve as communicating vessels: artists with public relations people, social scientists with businesspeople, writers with journalists, politicians with communicators, scientists with educators, workers with professionals, pornographers with psychologists, poor people with poor people. The social fabric would appear simultaneously fragmented and enriched by a web of sensitivities, languages, specializations, and life strategies that would, in turn, acquire a segmented visibility in the means of mass communication. The dispersing force would conspire with the solidity of democratic institutions in order to mediate, on the public level, the multiple fragmented demands emanating from that dispersion. Politicians would likewise have to professionalize in order to address the difficult task of creating an equilibrium between cultural diversity and social peace.

This cultural density would permit an equal relativization of both disenchantment and triumphalism. On one hand, emancipatory energies would encounter channels of sublimation in many varied spheres: the neighborhood community, creativity in whatever professional field, development in production and cultural consumption, etc. On the other hand, the fragmenting logic of the market and of instrumental rationality would, in these same spaces, possess an effective counterweight. While culture might well operate as an axis for relativizing cost-benefit rationality, it's also the case that this rationality would look to culture to consolidate itself (following the much-touted Japanese model). This tension of reciprocal uses between cultural consumption and the culture of consumption could constitute itself in a battlefield whose participants were perpetually disposed to come up with new ideas for mediation and transaction.

Generalized individualism would combine with the permanent search for peers in the micro-environment. Each person could thus be turned into an administrator-administratee, and administrative rationality could be internalized without threatening the diversity of relations. But once again, the masses of the excluded could become victims and disruptors. There, fragmentation redounds to the benefit of manipulation and violence.

Just as development allows the diversity of the private to combine with a public sphere that has strong, symbolic effectiveness, which processes demands from a wide range of social actors, so would democratic culture enrich itself via a "mode of widened secularization."

This "widened secularization" constitutes the optimistic scenario for culture for the upcoming years in South America. It would imply the development of two complementary tendencies: first, through redistributive policies, the greater political participation of less integrated actors, and the extension of the benefits of modernization to excluded social strata; and secondly, the diversified incorporation of cultural forms and symbols of identification that don't submit to instrumental reason or to the logic of the market.

It might be enough to project the first tendency as an effect of democratization's opening of new channels for political participation and making economic growth compatible with social equity. The combination of these factors could guarantee greater levels of social integration. The opening of channels of participation to emerging actors would amplify the spectrum of agreement and consequently augment the power of the most marginalized sectors' influence on decisive moments in the formulation of politics. The redistributive struggle would be more equilibrated, without deteriorating the general consensus required to guarantee social peace and political stability. This might be made viable through the combination of a series of actions: administrative decentralization with an effective decentralization of power and resources; a system of political parties capable of absorbing demands not represented in less organized groups; a parliament capable of legislating the use of public resources with redistributive effects; the management of political economy oriented towards expanding productive employment, and greater participation of the poor in orienting and executing social policies. Thus combining economic development and social integration would be the mainspring of a "secularization of solidarity" whose values of social integration and national development would have meaning and reality. Democracy would then have an expanded cultural support, granting it greater legitimation. The feeling of belonging to a national unity and to joint development projects would channel emancipatory energies towards an image of integrated modernity, of sustained overcoming poverty by way of gradual, positive changes. This same image could serve as a spring towards reestablishing values of responsibility and social solidarity within individual entrepreneurial agency. The gap between the excluded and the integrated would be gradually narrowed, and the meaning of national unity and social progress would be the best antidote to social violence, the fresh outbreak of fundamentalisms, and the fragmenting effects of the market.

To the degree that secularizing modernization impacts societies that are socially integrated and more politically participative, the field of culture and communication would have to be a legitimate receptacle for differentiation and individuation. An effect of the opening of markets for cultural goods and services is the amplification of symbols of identification and of collective referents of belonging. Democratic stability and social integration would also be the necessary substrata for a culture to transcend the restricted limits of instrumental reason and the exaltation of the market. The channels of social communication would enable the opening of public life to multiple forms of expression by diverse sociocultural actors. Urban art, neighborhood development groups, communication and computing networks, popular and classical theater, extracurricular education, currents for esotericism and personal growth, spaces for cultural promotion on television, city newspapers with community participation, sports activities in the neighborhoods, popular holidays, the expansion of countercultural proposals with access to public diffusion, peace conferences, folklore, the diffusion of vernacular cultures, diversified offers for the consumption of culture and communication: the options for differentiation within a context of amplified secularization would be rooted in all of these.

Within this field, technology could fill a function subordinated to personal development, which ever-increasing sectors could reach. The field of culture will likewise receive the creative reconfiguration of emancipatory dreams, turning the subversion of norms into a diversity of expressive norms, in order to counter the fragmenting effects of the market with multiple offers for group interaction. New public services would be created, incorporating the less integrated sectors into interactive computing networks, thus linking them with their distant peers. To the extent that costs decrease, national institutions for aiding in the production of popular videos and community radio stations will multiply. Extended education schools for adults will be created in order to disseminate codes for the use and consumption of new goods in the cultural and mass media markets. Public libraries will have terminals installed in homes and schools. A high dose of imagination and creativity will be destined to improve and expand cultural action. This action will consist of combining financial, tax, commercial, and technological instruments in order to optimize the access of distinct socioeconomic and sociocultural segments to the channels through which the society's messages circulate. The ongoing reduction in the size and costs of new cultural consumption and communication hardware and the reduction in operating costs and space requirements will permit a vast field of action for democratizing access to the cultural market.

Just as the hypothesis of violence might be apocalyptic, this scenario of cultural integration might be utopian. Once again, the exaggeration helps to visualize the limits within which the trajectory of possibility opens towards a future of uncertain signs.

Finally . . .

What's been put into relief here are the limiting images for diagnosis and the art of sleight of hand. The present tendencies aren't limited to disenchantment regarding the loss of emancipatory social mysticism and privatist-instrumental triumphalism. Such disenchantment and triumphalism are the limits within which many possible combinations coexist. They do not occupy the center of discourse. Rather, they signal its extremes. They are walls encircling the city, within which a multitude of symbols shift around and visions of the world compose an intricate mesh of collective sensitivities.

In the same way, in this anticipatory essay I have tried to sketch out images of the border. Let's not wait until one of them, whether utopian or hellish, is installed in the coming years. Rather, let's meet the mixture of these distinct components, for the weight of each element is currently unknowable. Diverse fundamentalisms, cultures of violence, the diversification of human environments and values, and new guidelines for coexistence will probably form part of the cultural dynamics in South America in the coming years. These pages have sought to suggest a game of limits and ingredients for the coming years, without getting into the material that establishes them or the combination that will bring them to life. Here the phantoms have been stepped up, while the real bodies that they encircle remain far from clear.

Between phantoms and real bodies, blessed mediations will save us from those extremes.

Notes

1 Likewise the models of so-called development discourse: proposals for rationalized development founded in the enlightened knowledge of some elites were based on the premise of development's necessary directionality toward the general welfare.

2 In Chile, Joaquín Lavín, with his orchestrated best-seller, *La Revolución Silenciosa* (The Silent Revolution); in the industrialized world, Fukuyama provided *The End of History and the Last Man* (1992) as the symbol of this new capitalist crusade.

3 I'm referring to spaces offering an alternative to a status quo of secularization founded on a technocratic pattern focused on modernization.

4 Here, it's necessary to resolve a long debate between enlightened "critics" and postmodern ones: although multiple wills for emancipation persist, they are dispersed, not subsumable to a "truncated" project of modernity.

5 Financial capitalism, an aspect of post-industrial capitalism, is characterized by a maximization of profits deriving more from the management of money as merchandise than from the production of physical merchandise. In financial capitalism, the value of financial transactions in the international markets in the present day world is many times greater than the value of investment and commerce.

3 ✳ Neither Apocalyptic nor Integrated
(Eight Debatable Paradoxes)

First Paradox: As Confusion Is Aired, Misery Overheats

The impact on the present cultural climate of technology, the globalization of the market, the dismantling of real socialism, the lack of engaging alternatives to development, and the eruption of a segmented society of masses have all become almost tedious to point out. For the disenchanted, a kind of cool confusion rules, softened through the shift from visceral experience to discourse. For the apocalyptic, the prophets of doom, there's the loss of the prestige that "blasting criticism" once gave them vis-à-vis the status quo. Their former fellow travelers have branded the few that are left as dramatists, thickheaded, obsessive, or, simply, out of place. Here, the tragicomic, recognizable outcome: negative thought no longer mobilizes students yet it's been captured in well-produced books, almost collectors' items, at inaccessible prices.

On the reverse of the same coin, the utopians experience a similar fate: simulacra of dialogue is the most they can aspire to in the court of "enlightened" public opinion. At this point in time, invocations such as "the universal unfolding of human potential" are attributed more to the dimensions of rhetoric and hysteria than to hope and history. Those who look at the few remaining apocalyptic and utopian thinkers as if they were a residue of chronic anachronisms assume a lack of clarity regarding the processes that regulate the world as almost one more piece of data. The idea that this lack of clarity doesn't matter is then incorporated into the metabolism. There would be some cynicism in this, yet not enough to be scandalous.

But this disenchanted tempering doesn't lower the volume for those who are miserable. Even as confusion is aired, misery keeps on overheating. Urban marginality, rural deterioration, the regressive distribution of income, the persistence of informal sectors — categories that aren't anachronistic at all — coexist, undiluted, with categories of stochastic complexity, multivariate processes, planning for uncertainty, comparative advantages, virtuous and vicious discontinuities. Those ominous realities that strengthen the discourse of the prophets of apocalypse are more shining than ever, while, paradoxically, the discourse invoking them sounds rather outdated. There could be a thousand explanations for this, yet one thing would be irrefutable and symptomatic: as confusion is assumed with growing disdain, misery's temperature rises.

Second Paradox: Now It Turns Out that Integration Disintegrates

All effective forms of social integration have probably generated, in their time, some degree of disintegration. But beyond this possible law about social nature, the currently disconcerting situation: in twenty years, the mechanisms of integration have acquired an exponentially multiplied speed, simultaneity, and coverage even as their disintegratory effects bear the same rhythm and exhaustiveness.

A benevolent interpretation would promote segmented integration as the solution for sustaining mass society and at the same time prevent any sacrifice of the modern appetite for individuality. The combination of crossed temporalities within a single society, where premoderns, moderns, and hypermoderns all live together, would be the new form of integrating without homogenizing. The new cultural-industrial complex would possess the virtue of respecting the tastes and sensibilities of individuals and groups incorporated as producers and consumers. This postmodern tribalization would be ethically sustainable in a postindustrial order where cultural fragmentation placidly rests on a stable, democratic political system, acceptably funded unemployment insurance, and citizenship status for all. But this doesn't even occur in the vast majority of so-called opulent cultures, where the "minor" problems are increasingly "major."

In our region, the flourishing cultural-industrial complex seems to promote new impetus for symbolic integration. But that impetus shatters against the opaque wall of social integration. The segmented access to new goods of communication and information maintains a great part of the society in a position of relative backwardness, and risks widening distances in terms of productivity levels, access to new markets, and the development of the capacity to adapt to change. On the one hand, there is the promise of greater integration through price reductions on new goods in the culture industry, whose malleability allows for penetrating different sociocultural scenes. On the other hand, new forms of cybernetic illiteracy threaten to close in on the ample contingent of Latin Americans who lack access to any form of computing.

Those who are most deprived of access might be consoled by the fact that speed and segmentation prevent anyone from ever managing to integrate completely. The disenchanted might console themselves with the certainty that integration no longer represents a positive value or utopian potential in itself and that the best thing is not to get one's hopes up. But beyond these justifications there emerges an inescapable phenomenon: never before has there been a greater combination of options for integration, via the communications revolution, the widening of markets, global interconnections, and cultural exchange. Never before has there been, either, greater disintegration: call it the crisis of development, the frustration of expectations for social mobility, gaps in productivity, fragmentation following the demobilization of the masses, the loss of collective referents, or a blurring of the future. The anti-psychiatrists' scandalous thesis that schizophrenia is a social production takes on a new figure as a metaphor for this double movement.

Third Paradox: Accumulation as Synchrony

Various events substantially change the industrial image of accumulation, associating it with constant and continual processes of productive investment. One of these is the rise of financial capitalism and its primacy over productive capitalism, especially since the boom of petrodollars in the 1970s. Another, the vertiginous, decisive, and hypercompetitive role that large businesses have assigned to technological innovations in order to ensure their survival and expansion. Another, the subordination of the rationality of endogenous development to the "rationality of insertion," within a world ruled by comparative dynamic advantages in a globalized mercantile order with high levels of uncertainty.

These three phenomena are only part of the architecture of a paradox that can be formulated as follows: the more we disconnect ourselves from the past, the more agile our possibilities for accumulation. The self-made man increasingly resembles a poker player: rather than the will to accumulation, the management of simultaneous combinations held in hand. It's no coincidence that game theory enters so strongly into economic theory today. The greater capital is to be integrally connected to the movement of capital around us — more than investments, operations, and even "gambles" or bets, more than an increment in the series, its diversification. Adaptation becomes the formula for persistence. In this, the prosperous businessperson from a rich country and the urban participant in the informal sector from a poor country mirror one another, although each one has a different fate.

Millions of springs for jumping into opulence, out of trickery, or into bankruptcy are created and closed off every day. The most profitable continuity is to continually attune oneself to this phenomenon. Swift, precise information is worth more than steel. This goes not only for economic investments: at least, in an analogous sense, new synchronic reason permeates politics, aesthetics, and a person's ties with the rest. *The Bonfire of the Vanities* has primacy over *The Waste Land,* the opportune alliance over the strategic proposal, the gallery over the museum. Only the ephemeral transcends. In order to progress, better erase the footprints, feeling no nostalgia or feeling a cheerful, light nostalgia.

The new modernity in underdevelopment, drunk on amnesia, looks to straighten itself out between its intoxicating air and its dynamic development. As if this dynamic equilibrium were always obliging it to keep on moving, advancing, inventing. Inertia tends to regression: more contamination, density, traffic, and alienation. More progress, greater energy in the flight forward is always needed to counter it. To distance oneself from the past is the war cry against entropy and stagnation. Like a gigantic factory, the Latin American metropolis only shows itself as productive when it is smoking. Centrifugal impulse and opening towards the exogenous are announced as the promise of a new identity. The absurd prejudice is imposed: that disconnecting the tube that connects us with our own history is the easiest way of synchronizing ourselves with the constant movement coming from outside. The promise of new identity is not accumulative.

But whose identity, if the substance of biography has been erased to ease this adjustment, and there's no voice of one's own left, no decision capable of self-affirmation from outside of the magnetic field of imitative inertia? And it's necessary to recognize that many of those who don't accede to this field of real and symbolic consumption seek only to forget what they have been and accede to the material forms that make viable those profoundly styleless lifestyles. In this transition from an ideal of modernity made of its own singular synthesis to a new transnationalized ideal that seemingly enjoys a rootless contingency, whose specific place on the map already turns out to be indifferent, what happens with our territory? How, following this loss of memory, shall we return to question our desire for modernity?

Surely there's some attraction to the idea that learning is unlearning, to the invitation to contemporaneity, to the vitality of forgetting. Yet do we propose this lightness as an aesthetic for life?

Fourth Paradox: The More We Develop, the More Critical Does Our Quality of Life Become

Is it worthwhile, or not, to clamber onto the train of this modernity, which is so freighted with corrosive effects on our quality of life? The progressive frequency of environmental and psychosocial catastrophes in our cities makes the terms modernization and quality of life seem increasingly disharmonious in the silent evaluations that we all formulate. The historical equation is inverted so that improving the quality of life no longer appears as a positive-dependent variable of the process of modernization.

For some decades now, we have identified modernization with expansive dynamics, so that despite its many costs and sacrifices, it would allow greater collective access to the satisfaction of basic needs. These basic needs would include more modern employment, better incomes, greater access to goods and services, growing rates of schooling, better attention to health for the city's entire population, the expansion of social security, and prospects for better housing. But the frequency and gravity of environmental catastrophes, the social costs provoked by the new patterns of open economies, and the nervous wear and tear that human life entails amid modernity all wind up destroying this positive correlation between modernization and quality of life. The notion of quality of life is less and less reducible to rates of schooling, life expectancy at birth, or the reduction of infant mortality rates. It extends to dimensions with strong territorial, environmental, and psychosocial overtones. The catastrophe displaces quality of life towards other objects: our air, rhythm of life, proximity or distance from nature, our historical rootedness.

For those who were and are integrated, as well as for those few who used to be apocalyptic but subsequently converted and are now well off, as well as for those who are ambiguous (a group that includes many formerly apocalyptic, and a few formerly integrated burn-outs who subsequently converted), quality of life currently problematizes this equilibrium of compensations amid the newest modernizing wave. The waste or dregs of progress is so very visible in the gray-black color that grips the contaminated air in Mexico City, Santiago de Chile, or São Paulo, that it is very hard to avoid a constant calculation of the pros and cons of development and modernity. For some time now, an inversely proportional relation between two variables, proximity to the urban nucleus and quality of life, has been insinuated in the social imagination.

This inversion of terms floats in the air: the term "quality of life" becomes very conflictive for those who'd rather clamber onto the chariot of progress. This chariot not only crosses the city. It also disfigures it. Multiple congestion isn't a good stimulus for opening the present towards the desiring imagination. Utopian invention, its modern version included, tends to see itself as having been cornered as space becomes tighter and denser. To avoid apocalyptic premonitions, it's better to think that as this density borders on catastrophe, the question for survival irradiates towards questioning the meaning of our historical options, thus turning to activate the search for new horizons.

Fifth Paradox: Thirsting for Projects but Lacking a Foundational Metaphysics for Action

It isn't easy, these days, to think of a concept of action that can help us to reconceive ourselves as true historical subjects. The loss of repertoire comes from many flanks. We shall look at only a few examples.

The Hegelian matrix, by virtue of which we were formerly able to recognize and progressively complete ourselves by recognizing a world that we were progressively completing and improving, now seems unsustainable. Now the world seems to be completing itself through others, and coming apart for us. Discontinuity, as much in our manner of articulating ourselves as in reality itself, makes it difficult to take hold of the idea of synthesis between the subject and history.

I'm referring not just to the much noted collapse of socialism, but to the weight of forces that regulate the world order, from which local orders are also regulated: one could speak of technological impact, the market, the transnationalization of culture. Could we feel, however remotely, that we are crafting some of these forces, and are responsible for their effects, or that we are the humble subjects of a dialectics of history? The new logic neutralizes, but also seduces: to intervene is no longer to subvert but to combine.

With respect to the matrix of Guevara, the working class hero and Fanon: Who now could resolutely throw themselves into proclaiming anti-colonial, anti-imperialist, anti-bourgeois action, knowing that these models of "consistent struggle" are hardly even filmic? The only current example of real confrontation with the world order is called Hussein. Only there do we find, in recent years, a negation of the North and West with real global impact, signed and sealed by an irrationality that turns our stomachs, whose messianic violence reeks of holocaust. Would we be disposed to assume this only real model as our own?

And regarding the matrix of radical action, where the negation of the world runs alongside our personal surrender: the vengeance of the shattered, the mad bomber, the acrobat, and the anti-urban now provoke more curiosity than identification. Artaud, Burroughs, Hendrix and Co. aren't models of imitation but, at most, objects for study.

Which model of action should we adopt, then, if we want to preserve the idea that in action there is something that goes beyond its immanence and its contingency? Where can we find today, in relation to any of the above-mentioned matrices, an exemplary action that allows the defense, as epic or lyric, of action itself as manifestation of a meaning? Curiously, we continue to inhabit a world (and a discourse) that is hyperkinetic, and that looks to action for justification, a world in which the word "project" is repeated like a twentieth century mantra. Homo faber inhabits us now more than ever, but chasing and biting its own tail.

Sixth Paradox: Seeking the Centrality of the Peripheral

Facing this crisis of models of action, of integrations that disintegrate, accumulation without a past, airing confusion and overheated misery, the image of a possible revolution likewise seems displaced, less prefigured as the center of the future, more projected into the periphery of the present. Now the image of a possible revolution is also marked by synchrony: it seeks to give expression to simultaneous worlds, in the margins of an unacceptable general order, whether postindustrial, industrial, or preindustrial, to create pockets of utopia. The crystallization of this image of qualitative change aims not towards a redemptive future, but towards the gaps or hollow spaces freed up in the present, in its "dynamic complexity."

In this tonic of contiguous orders, some exalt the rationality of a world defined as popular, holistic and in solidarity, situated in the periphery of the cities of undeveloped countries and in rural areas. Such a world vision denies dominant rationality without dissolving it or inverting its hegemony. The invocation of gender, sexuality, and non-hegemonic cultures also gets strengthened. Still, in these invocations there's no pretension of passing on to hegemony, but rather to living on under the very sign of resistance. Others would rather bet on spaces that the logic of the market of cultural goods or the reigning sensibility cannot recover: art-actions, "installations," or swift "interventions" in the everyday bone and gristle of the cities, fragments of a cryptic aesthetic that decides in an almost tribal fashion its own codes for interpretation, thus making itself incomprehensible to those who don't belong to the tribe.

Others resolutely bet on personal change by mining esoteric veins which likewise possess a synchronic character. The Tarot, the *I Ching*, meditation, astrology, runic stones, biodance, Jungianism, and Tai Chi don't seem to exclude but rather to bring people together in an "other" mentality. It has nothing to do with adhering to a single tradition or school, but rather with discovering, amid that vast offer of search options, the best combination for exorcising, on the personal plane, the full weight of social alienation.

In those attempts to establish relative autonomies, rather than to pull down the system's structures, the revolution is no longer conceived in terms of great temporal changes. The revolution is recognized as small and significant changes in space. Versions are smuggled in from synchronic rationality, turning the esoteric into the exoteric, tribal withdrawal into the folds of this extroverted urbanity at the century's end. The long voyage from Genesis to Apocalypse is compressed in everyday experiences, joined up with that "other reality" of the periphery where vulnerability is exacerbated and conjured on a daily basis. Graffiti, the rituals of witches (esoteric rituals) or the base community (grassroots action) are all equally provisional. The alternative is announced in slender places, slim gaps, tepid disorders, where the symbolic reach is already almost sufficient.

But for whom, and for how many?

*Seventh Paradox: The More We Escape from
Alienation, the More We Return to It*

And in the middle of these forces in tension, the logic of performance and of the market also cut into the traffic on the heavily traveled roads towards emancipation. Then a total discourse appears, full of new hierarchical relations, evaluating each of us in a new "ranking" of the quality of life: gyms, tennis at hand, weekend psychotherapies, workshops for facilitating communication and expression, workplace services for weighing the anxieties of its members and reducing tension at work. A whole new market emerges to match the expectations related to quality of life and its optimization, with a culture of optimization alongside "healthy growth," personal development, overcoming our karma.

Our atavistic spirit of piety doesn't get conjured away. To the contrary: it is revived in workshops for personal, spiritual, and communicative growth. New Age sensitivity, which gives us the possibility of refreshing our utopian vocation by way of a holistic narrative with more light and more sex appeal, is furiously incorporated into the culture industry and the market exchange of rapidly obsolescing goods and services. Offers of emancipation take people's busy lives into account, considering the possibility that they might be able to devote some time at night or on weekends. Instead of thinking of changing one's life, better to avoid getting overheated from the air. Chaplin's *Modern Times* can displace alienated labor onto the cult of personal development: a rationalization of time accompanies the in-between options through which we resist alienation and seek to humanize ourselves. We run from our hour of gestalt therapy to a tennis match, from there to a conference on family gatherings. All this, without taking our eyes from the minute hand on the watch.

It wouldn't be strange to expect a new form of represssive desublimation (an expression that apocalyptic ones cherish): quality of life as an ideal that internally reproduces a new hyperkinesis for achieving the maximum number of points in this incipient ladder of "personal development." No one debates the pertinence and urgency of new spaces for personal growth, for disseminating, on a planetary scale, an ecological mentality and a full reconsideration regarding what is meant by quality of life. But neither should we become pseudo-ecological fanatics of asepsis, or go around, puffy-cheeked, preaching spiritual vigor. We have acquired, in our stride, tripped up by modernity, a quota of hedonism and taste for autonomy that we cannot renounce, which inoculates us against these new versions of the fakir, the Calvinist, or the utopian of total surrender.

Eighth Paradox: For Consistency's Sake,
Dare to Be Inconsistent

Amid these paradoxes — from which I do not exempt myself — I am sizing up heterodox formulas and seeking through language so many other paradoxical expressions in order to try to come up with a foundation for action, a "link to otherness" with the world, or at least to sketch out an approach. I try out rhetorical combinations that are more ingenious than effective, and thus I make ambiguous references to a fecund disenchantment, menacing resignation, healthy irony, subverted inconsistency. In the end, there's nothing to think about as a new foundation for universalizable actions.

Skepticism might be the diet of intelligence, but it shouldn't be intelligence itself. Overstaying that visit could turn into a lamentable excess of coherency, a new form of obesity. Better, perhaps, to seek another form of coherence in this synchronic temper of the contemporary where nothing is too coherent, which seems and surely is a contradiction.

But it's not a question of renouncing hope for another form of integration, or for the possibility of an action whose transformative meaning reinforces our fantasies of the world. Rather, the intent is to recognize, in the first place, that these fantasies have yet to redefine themselves and that we can't, at the same time, suspend all action while we process that redefinition. Perhaps being consistent requires submerging oneself in a decided inconsistency: to celebrate this orphanhood of comprehensive narratives and to visit, without prejudice, some partial narratives that may not totally convince us, but could pertain to an itinerary whose outcome is clearly uncertain. Why not explore the discourses of difference, the interstices of politics, esotericism and its proliferation of meanings, symbolic action, popular culture, suggestive intuitions, spasmodic revolt, economies of the displaced, the hermeticism of vernacular and postmodern tribes, passion's reasons, intimist conversation? And why not do it with childish curiosity, without expectations of surrender or performance, with shameless vitality? Why not venture to create a bit of literature with the surroundings and with one's own biography, even if only to shuffle the cards all over again?

Neither apocalyptic nor integrated.

4 ✹ Realism and Revolt, Twenty Years Later
(Paris 1968–Santiago de Chile 1988)

May 1968 in France survives as a model and as a myth of contemporary revolt, as what has happened and as what cannot be repeated. Its inscription in our memory is therefore ambivalent. It provides us with the living example of a social movement, more intensive than extensive, capable of putting into play all the will for massive rupture that political pragmatism postpones. Suddenly, that May in France—and from there, Germany, Italy, North America, Japan—erupted into the field of the public, politicizing everything in a politicization that would be, in turn, a radical change in life. "To break" was the heroic verb in which existence found an almost aesthetic justification. The bridges of metaphor, action, spontaneous insurrection were built for the gap between the real and the impossible, between desire and its realization. Sufficient to consider the citizen as artist, and politics as generosity. The paving stone that leapt, almost through osmosis, from pavement to barricade and from there was thrust towards an unforeseeable future, became part of the catapult for getting to the bottom of one's own, suddenly collective, dreams. For an instant, nothing was discarded as delirious. Even the old passionate utopias of

Charles Fourier were parried about, in that agenda for the future which was being remade from day to day, in the heat of events.

Collective memory, which better retained the happy marriage of aesthetics and politics, softened the dose of violence, sweat, or impatience that accompanied those laborious days. Later, the new folds of power, always more plastic than their opponents, put the bolts on the revolt. In the industrialized world the bourgeois order regained control with no showy display of physical force. Of course, there were changes: the authoritarianism of educational institutions and of families was rigorously questioned — an interrogation that, at least in France and Germany, came to form part of common sense. Sexuality, already quite emancipated for the time, became even more liberated. Marxism found itself obliged to revise its principles. But the bourgeois order did not die. To the contrary, it widened its tolerance, even integrating the apparently indigestible: it integrated the productive rationalization of late capitalism with the growing differentiation in the field of subjectivity.

May went by. And June, and the summer, and many years now. Uncertain revolutions, toppled or distorted, peopled some non-industrialized corners of the earth, while the First World maintained a status quo of conservatives, liberals, and social democrats respectively venturing changes so slight that the optic of the revolt stigmatized them as "shameful continuism." The old revolutionaries of May then became pro-Chinese; anti-Stalinism emptied its currents into neoliberalism. Taking advantage of the new left's self-critical tendency, the market apologists, with their ongoing project of cultural hegemony, engulfed large contingents of people who felt deceived by the revolt.

What in Europe seemed an ideological defeat, in our corner of the world was produced with all the violence not exposed in the European capitals.[1] There, the consolidation of capitalism claimed no victims, or so few that they were lost under the basic structure. There was, of course, cultural crisis, and perhaps there still is, although it is resolved between "civilized people": political changes are sublimated into intellectual fashions, and the growing internationalization of the market has permitted the invisible hand to be withdrawn from the coatrack, clothed with new energies. The slogan "technology anywhere, any time, for any need" inaugurates the obsolescence of the conflict. The noisy revolt has nothing to do with Fukuyama's *End of History*, with that implacable march. Even as the imposition of this asepsis leads conflicts to disappear under the euphoria of the market, courtesy is violently shattered once again, not because of political confrontations between the centers, but because of irrepressible regional and/or fundamentalist wars, call them Hussein or Sarajevo.

In Chile, as in other countries of Latin America, this silent revolution has been preceded by terror and the brutal colonization of bodies and souls. The chronology of that cultural change, the so-called end of the old struggle between the classes, opens with the physical crushing of collectively figured dreams and socially undertaken projects. Only the cynicism of technocrats and businesspeople could induce the disremembering of this sinister origin which is, at the same time, a style and a trajectory. In these regions of ours, the narrative of the revolt was not attacked in a civilized fashion, that is, through the politics of debilitation and disrepute, but with all the archaism that underlies the modern: with the cross and the sword, with the guillotine, and the ideology and practice of internal war.

The revolt of May was, at the same time, denouement and élan for the narrative of radical change. That paradox marks its ambiguous position in our present moment. As denouement, the unexpected — explosive, implosive — succeeded just as the ephemeral failed. May was poetry: a narrative which hoped to crystallize what it evokes, which flourishes only in its failure.

But to what extent has the defense of that May, or better yet, of the values underlying it and the critical judgments implied, been erased by distance and the passage of time? Would it be anachronistic or out of place, perhaps, to question the politics of capitalist power, crowd morality, the pious spirit, authoritarian culture, reproduction of conventional family values, competitiveness and social injustice, the rhetoric of conventional politics? Would it be irrelevant to carry into programmatic discussion the connection between political repression and the repression of desire, between private property and sexual discrimination, between science and the will to rule, between ideology and self-interest, between the control of bodies and the control of consciousness?

We know very well that none of this has lost its current importance, and that such questionings can't be discarded as irrelevant. On the contrary, in different countries of Latin America, first the experience of military power, then the regressive effects of the crises and the adjustments, have made those distinct faces of domination both very evident and unmanageable. The strategy of maximizing the moderate, making explicit the implicit, shows (at the same time, and perhaps to one's own disadvantage) that arriving at that repressive extreme constitutes no more than making evident the previously hidden, which at the moment of revolt was deprived of its most attractive task, that of unmasking. If May in France deciphered the system's hypocrisy (that is, it turned that hypocrisy into irrefutable truths), in Chile the disguised has been self-revealed with such absolute aplomb that there is no longer anything left into which to delve. Here we're presented with the violent, classist character of power: liberal ideology's repressive potential, the alliance between the State and the capitalist project, between morality and repression, the psychological dimensions of the exercise of authority, and the manipulation of unconscious phantoms for the purpose of social discipline. The military regime realized all of these with such obviousness that no opponent would surpass its ability to establish the fallacy of bourgeois peace.

The preceding has made possible a perverse dialectic. On one hand, the course of events confirmed the truthfulness of the critical contents with which May contests the system. But on the other hand, that same confirmation rendered the movement impractical for two reasons: because nothing is left to be unmasked (and, by the same measure, the revolt loses one of its principle challenges and gratifications), and because nothing can really be broken (on maximizing capitalist power in all its facets, or on widening its capacity for integration, the revolt becomes an impotent caricature). The dynamic of liberalism, even the spurious versions that it acquires in Latin America, contested the dynamic of the revolt with its captivating dialectic of unmasking and rupture.

Late capitalism has turned out not to be entropic, but elastic. Entropy apparently resides in the critical spirit: we all know how to practice the art of suspicion, yet it doesn't mobilize us to rebel. We all know that the real or symbolic outcome of breaking is a murder, whether of God, of the father, or of the bourgeois. Even so, we doubt that this murder will efficiently eradicate relations marked by domination. The condition of lucidity coexists with being overloaded; our dexterity is confused with our clumsiness. None of us has any confidence in the recourse of or to utopia, yet we also know that without utopia, pragmatic logic will keep on administering our cultural dramas as if they were economic problems. And they will continue, with their unperturbed stride, equating the terrain of power with technical operations.

Facing this perplexity, we evoke May 1968. Isn't pragmatism and realism therefore contested, showing its reactionary bias? Wasn't there an allusion to the play of alliances between economy and culture, power and technical skill, the dominant morality and the phantasmal fear of chaos?

The fact is that nothing remains to be unmasked: yet is this sufficient cause to demotivate the revolt? Or might it not oblige a reformulation of the very model of revolt?

On one hand, total exteriorization of the system reduces the political debate to the criteria of effectiveness: convenient alliances, inadequate tactics, situational positions, lesser evils, viable negotiations. Everybody knows what there is to know. The denunciation that hangs over the institutions, and over the terror exercised by some of them, is ratified by those in opposition, while the supporters don't change their position. The "oppositional gesture" — be it the street demonstration, the university sit-in, the hunger strike, the vigil, banging on pots and pans — would seem self-consuming, incapable of getting past the fence of self-reference. Everybody knows everything and nobody convinces anyone. May becomes winter in waking memory.

But the will to break ought to seek, imperiously, new forms. Pragmatic solutions founded in negotiation and political realism invite the revolt to exceed them. That invisible revolt, which cannot be located in the political aspect or in what the political parties offer, perhaps doesn't correspond to the model of the "occupied street," to the dialectics of the paving stone and of unmasking.

May's revolt was, perhaps, the greatest (and last) expression of the politicization of the will to break, a will with which we still can identify, albeit partially and in reflecting on what can't be recovered. The university went into the street, confronted the police, put the government into check. Laborers and the working classes, the exploited and the repressed, joined in, expectant, with the street's living theater. Young people made their generational identity the battleground for power, and not merely a confrontation with teachers in the classroom or with their parents in the living room. Politics, clearly overtaken by utopian will, was forced to widen its confrontation scenarios. At present, however, few believe in politics as a vehicle for radical change. The ruling realism has been emptied of utopias and expectations for structural change. The revolt has correspondingly lost its right to exteriorization. The will to rupture, that the French May crystallized in the eruption of "the other" in the middle of the public — fully politicizing the other — has been made interstitial, peripheral, fragmentary, partial, or local.

Neither curses or dreams can be scrawled on the wall of political reconstruction. Only formulas for negotiation, retractions, terribly sensible appeals, variations on a single theme. Politics has lost its totalizing range, which might be good, but with it, part of its seductive power. Nobody believes that in the short or middle term it can recover its capacity for giving meaning to citizenship. What remains is a sensation of political simulacrum in which, with distinct nuances and in the interest of achieving modest gains, the actors of the regime and of the opposition intervene. At this point, the political news is more centered on performance than on value: the clumsiness of one, the ingenuity of the other, the effectiveness of the third, the anachronism of the fourth, the convincing quality of the fifth, the tactical blindness of the other one, the sixth, and for the seventh, the smell of the goal. It's not that the field of politics is any less real for intensifying its technical-theatrical component. But it's only as real as "the persistence of the same," a game already played, which offers only the possibility of interpreting or adjusting the moves, without breaking or disrupting them.

Given the loss of politics' interpellative potency, how to reorient the model of the revolt so that the will to rupture can continue to be exercised? Suppose the political revolt, as collective imagination and as effective outcome, sealed its fate when the last students of May, real or metaphorical, French or Latin American, let the paving stone slip from their hands. Rather than risking or tossing it towards an uncertain future, suppose they returned to their classrooms. In that case, what model of revolt are we in the process of gestating now?

Ultimate values could remain for us from May 1968 although with distinct forms of elaborating and fleshing them out. Maybe these forms and those procedures don't provoke and produce, in their turn, other ultimate values. Aren't the utopias that the street demonstrator had in mind in Paris 1968 different from those of a community organizer in 1988? How is that difference explained? We know all too well what separates us from those who supported Pinochet's regime. There are no secrets on that ground. There's a total exteriorization of the conflict: everybody knows everything and nobody convinces anyone. But what separates us from what we were, from the examples that once were, but no longer are worth imitating? What can we offer or generate in lieu of the political roads of totalization, the Statist narrative, and/or the masses as the producers of meaning?

Suddenly we discover that "difference" signifies and that, under a certain perspective, aspiring governors can remain together on the same side of the dividing line on the political map. On the other side of that dividing line there remains, provisionally, a huge question mark, because governments, just like political classes, coincide in realist criteria: in the centrality of performance in the political and of the political in the cultural, and in the eradication of the will to break outside the limits of the political game. This puts them, from the optic of difference, within a shared universe of discourse, where the narrative of political totalization continues to dominate.

But what if this political totalization were turned into a synonym of preservation — that is, irreconcilable with the will to break? What place can the latter occupy? The subject and the predicate, that in May of 1968 are assembled in a single sentence, have separated from one another. The revolt is left helpless, then, orphaned of a narrative.

What is, or should be, the narrative of a generation that lived the experience of the military coup in Chile or Argentina during adolescence, or that lived through unrest in the university, and now, with democracy restored, doesn't identify itself with the party system of political practice? What is or should be the narrative of a generation that lived the myth of May in France, the hippie movement, political revolt as the "libidinization" of the public sphere, and facing all this oscillates between skepticism and nostalgia? What is or should be the narrative of a generation that embraced dreams of moral and social rupture from an eruption of the passionate and the popular in the political, but now surprises itself by reproducing the fears and zeal for security that it initially condemned? What is or should be the narrative of a generation that once fantasized about becoming marginal, proletarian, guerrillas, ascetic, or orgiastic, and now regards these same fantasies as stereotypica — a generation that flocked to the banner of the Great Cause and now looks to small interstices and final peripheries to reconquer the new life?

May should remain as a spirit of revolt, as scenification and/or materialization. We don't seek the unmasking function in its vestiges. Nor do we seek political totalization. Metamorphosing it into other kinds of crystallization is necessary to give it currency.

"To break" has surely been turned into a verb without yesteryear's magic. Deferred to the past and to the future, it is also deprived of the present. This distances us from May just as reality is distanced from myth. We can't play at pretending it's May. No theatrical capacity is available in that direction. The difference ventures out, taking roads that are humbler, not as massive and perhaps more dispersed, where the cultural, the local, the molecular, the peripheral are more rewarding than the political, the national, the integrated, the center. The images become more urgent than the definitions, the expression more revealing that its contents. The hermeneutic of symptoms is turned into the perspective from where reality is interpreted.

But there's nothing, from that perspective, to be unmasked. The body is not understood as hidden, or as work's demiurge. Rather, the body is now set upon the very surface of work, stretched and wounded, doubled and shamelessly exalted. This embodiment becomes evident in the preoccupation with form, texture, appearance ("essential" appearance), in the de-ideologization of the alternative or of the different, in the distrust for the dialectic of integration, whether highly cultured or savage, European or our own, or more serious yet, from the left or from the right.

This generation doesn't know the paving stone. Exteriorization is its problem, and its search. It has verified — or intuited? — that the real exteriority of political totalization that occurred under the dictatorships, negating itself as the possibility of revolt. The public was closed off. Expression ceased to be a right and a practice.

Something irreversibly changed. What uncertainty! Twenty years is more than nothing. Feverish glances set afire the landscape that they once tried to illuminate. Now recently, perhaps, the Nietzschean challenge of the death of God comes to life: let's seize our orphanhood instead of letting ourselves be overwhelmed by it. Indeed, May counterattacks. Let's get real. Breaking — it's possible.

Notes

This article, written during the second-to-last years of the military government in Chile, has been slightly updated following changes in the political map of that country.

1   In Mexico, the student revolts of 1968 had their chilling culmination in the massacre of Tlatelolco.

5 ❀ What Is Left Positive from Negative Thought?
A Latin American Perspective

Without attempting an exhaustive revision of critical theory or negative thought as conceived and developed in its moment by some exponents of the Frankfurt School, the following pages seek to establish analytical links between the contributions or dilemmas of negative thought and the challenges that critical reflection currently confronts in Latin America.[1] Such an exercise requires being (at least) somewhat critical of critical theory, especially in light of decisive phenomena such as the crisis of socialism in events, in ideas, and in the dissolution of a revolutionary social imagination that in past decades, for many intellectuals, managed to articulate a commitment to radical social change in the region.

The present chapter opens with a summary of some elements of critical theory and negative thought from the Frankfurt School, whose rescue or questioning could turn out to be important right now, in light of the phenomena noted above. These elements are then confronted with the crisis of the revolutionary referent in Latin America. Finally, some implications are formulated regarding possible connections between negative thought and the current critical function of the social sciences in our countries. These possible connections appear in the light of the crisis of Latin American development and the theoretical and practical search for alternative modes and approaches to development.

Negative Thought and Critical Theory: Elements
to Recall with Affection, Irritation, or Worry

Critical theory and the moment of negation

The critical theory that the Frankfurt School developed some decades ago tried to reformulate the functions and meanings of social theory. Keen to link social theory to an emancipatory ideal of modern humanism, it resorted to the dialectical concept of negation, from there seeking to negate (to object to, to contest) the relations of domination ruling in a "non-free" world.

But this moment of negation is complex and only can be understood by taking into account the three meanings that Frankfurt School philosophers ascribe to it, which they scarcely bother to clarify: the negation of pure theory, that is, working towards a reflection capable of transcending the world and closely identifying with the collective struggle for the expansion of real liberties; the problematization of that close identification between critical theory and the commitment to the real transformation of the structures of domination; and the negation of the existing order of things, which implies, on the one hand, challenging society and its forms of coercion and, on the other hand, affirming the possibilities which are contained and repressed by that same society.

Negation is, in short, the mobilizing exercise of criticism. It is by means of negation that things are revealed in their capacity for being other than the way that they appear to us, susceptible to profound unmasking and radical transformation: "To comprehend reality," indicates Marcuse, "means to comprehend what things really are, and this in turn means rejecting their mere factuality. Rejection is the process of thought as well as of action."[2] Not very different from this is the following, more hermetic meaning: "Negation plays a crucial role in philosophy. The negation is double-edged—a negation of the absolute claims of the prevailing ideology and of the brash claims of reality."[3]

The moment of negation in critical theory can also be understood as the relativization and contextualization of the objects upon which it reflects. This means that what we think about takes on greater clarity when we think about it in interaction with a combination of relations which that same object establishes with others, whether other objects or other subjects. The object of our reflection is thus explained in a frame of contradictions and is left, in turn, exposed in the falsity of its claims to the absolute: "Philosophy," says Horkheimer, "takes existing values seriously but insists that they become parts of a theoretical whole that reveals their relativity."[4]

In a similar sense, Adorno looks to understand criticism as contextualization put into perspective when he indicates that dialectic "criticism retains its mobility in regard to culture by recognizing the latter's position within the whole. Without such freedom, without consciousness transcending the immanence of culture, immanent criticism itself would be inconceivable: the spontaneous movement of the object can be followed only by someone who is not entirely engulfed by it."[5] With this, Adorno looks to turn the critical attitude itself into an object of critical thought. He contextualizes critical theory, showing its tense relation with the dominant culture: this relation is where he believes that the necessity of critical theory's defining itself as distinct from gregarious culture is discovered. Then he postulates the necessary independence that this critical vision should maintain with respect to the dominant culture, for if this difference did not exist, criticism would identify with the status quo, and this identification would leave no space for the progress of freedom.

It's important to prove that in Horkheimer's meaning as much as in Adorno's, critical theory understands negation as the constitutive moment of dialectical thought, by means of which this thought manages to de-ideologize itself, to situate itself outside of the "temptation to appearances," to capture the reality of the moment as a moment within reality. Dialectical negation thus becomes, in its turn, the decisive moment of critical thought, in which the mediate is worked out behind the immediate, the presence of the all, behind the part, and the non-absolute of a reality, behind the deceitful appearance of the absolute.

One might think that critical theory repeats the old dualism between hidden essence and deceitful appearance. But the tension between appearance versus essence here has two connotations that in no way refer to metaphysical dualism. In the first place, appearance constitutes a contradictory moment of essence within itself, an incomplete part of its own movement. Appearance is not, as in Platonism, the realm of the false or of the corrupt, but the road that essence itself travels (and crystallizes) in order to move forward, completing and historicizing itself. In this, critical theory is indebted to Hegelian dialectic. In the second place, the criticism of appearance should be understood as part of the criticism of totalitarianism and fetishization. What is objectionable, then, is the character of reification and ideology that appearance acquires. Not as mere "falsehood" in the Platonic sense, but as manipulation and alienation, as false consciousness and keen perception simultaneously: the expression of a will to domination that presents the existing conditions of domination as eternal.

Critical theory — and negative thought, more forcefully and with greater specificity — recognizes the world as not free, as that which isn't really as it is, or that is given only in an incomplete way.[6] This is evident where Marcuse argues that "Dialectical thought starts with the experience that the world is unfree, that is to say, man and nature exist in conditions of alienation, exist as 'other than they are.'"[7] Marcuse sees in Hegel's dialectic the most important referent for making reason a way of seeing the world in its "incompleteness," that is, as a world that incubates a yet-unrealized freedom, and whose movement necessarily exceeds its present moment — its appearance: "The matters of fact that make up the given state of affairs, viewed in the light of reason, become negative, limited, transitory — they become perishing forms within a comprehensive process that leads beyond them."[8]

In this way the act of unveiling reason is, at the same time, the act of dialectically negating the world. The emancipation of humanity is contained, behind appearance, in humanity itself, and reason's task is to break the circle of appearance in order to mobilize the world for the sake of its own emancipation. That is the will that animates critical thought, and also its enlightened matrix, in the proper meaning of the term. This happy coincidence endures, in negative thought, as long as happiness endures in the midst of misfortune. The emancipatory function of unveiling, which the Frankfurt School awards to reason, is immediately distorted by an old reactive trauma that reduces unveiling to an all-pervasive suspicion of all that is irrational, instrumental or mystical. The precautionary obsession concludes by expelling that will to freedom from the terrain of critical thought.

The gradient of negation

In principle, dialectical negation is negation of negativity, that is, refutation of the alienated, the repressive, the not-free, and at the same time, affirmation of the possibilities of overcoming that which is refuted. Dialectical thought defends itself against the alienation that it attributes to the world: it defends hope (present, in thought) and utopia (future, in the world, but never closed or predetermined). Nonetheless, thought should also protect itself from the "spurious" freedoms and "false hopes" of the reified world (which is alienated, not free). For Marcuse, the amalgam of freedoms and subjection of industrial society requires freedom to show itself as opposition to current progress. It's doubtless a problem for freedom, to have to appear under the form of the negation of progress. For Marcuse, freedom is affirmed, then, as a break in the line of capitalist progress — that is, as liberation. In this sense, and in contrast to other more despairing Frankfurt School philosophers, the negative character of freedom does not, for Marcuse, contradict the possibility of freedom. This is as evident in his battle text, *An Essay on Liberation*,[9] as in some earlier passages: "The total mobilization of society against the ultimate liberation of the individual, which constitutes the historical content of the present period, indicates how real is the possibility of this liberation."[10]

According to Adorno and Horkheimer, "the cultivation of 'hopes' in the very midst of false totality is a form of complicity and collaboration with the oppression and repression of totalitarian societies today. Only the renunciation of hope can, paradoxically, permit hope itself to survive amid all that continuously denies it."[11] This dramatic contradiction will be, at the same time, the identifying mark and gravestone for negative thought. By means of this operation, a range of features are attributed to that world filled with negativity. Among these features are the perverse capacity to absorb hopes and utopias, to neutralize their transformational potential, and to convert them into ideologies of preservation. By means of this operation, then, critical thinking begins to chase and bite its own tail: its lucidity becomes its excess. Philosophy is restricted to a kind of attitude which is extremely consistent and extremely bare. Nothing is left to it, but to act — with action as attack and disturbance — in a world that philosophy itself has previously qualified as impermeable to all disturbance. In this way, critical thought is more gesture than action, more symbolic than effective. Its pessimism can be understood — and thus defended — as a form of provocation, although it necessarily, according to the very pessimism of negative thinkers, bounces against the thick layer of the false consciousness of the social. To evade its reification, criticism must infinitely duplicate itself as criticism of criticism, and criticism of criticism of criticism, and so on, successively.

"Reason" should be negated by non-mystified reason in order not to fall back into a metaphysics of history. The criticism proposed by Adorno and Horkheimer is very consistent and lucid regarding the concept of historical necessity forged by Enlightenment: such criticism doesn't aim to overcome Enlightenment, but rather to protect it from its own totalitarian risk: "Its [Enlightenment's] untruth does not consist in what its romantic enemies have always reproached it for: analytical method, return to elements, dissolution through reflective thought; but instead in the fact that for enlightenment the process is always decided from the start."[12] Nietszche had already arrived at the conclusion that modern Reason is contradictory on this point, since on the one hand it proclaims the historical and ethical necessity of the autonomy of its subjects, while on the other hand, turning it into ethical and historical necessity subsumes all true desire for emancipation within a universal law, in which no autonomy is possible. Nietszche saw in this contradiction the craftiness of the "crowd spirit" at work behind the metanarratives of modernity: the dialectic of Enlightenment winds up guaranteeing, behind its liberational appearance, the imposition of a crowd morality. But Adorno and Horkheimer are closer to Weber than to Nietszche, for they are alarmed that the uses of reason are restricted to the deployment of a formal rationality that annihilates subjectivity by way of the mechanism of instrumental rationalization. Finally, Marcuse synthesizes these two critics of Enlightenment with an inevitable question that Enlightenment itself is condemned to leave unanswered: "How can slaves, who don't even know that they are enslaved, free themselves?"[13]

The reaction of Frankfurt School thinkers to this theoretical-practical problem is anything but uniform. On one extreme, Marcuse himself sought to break the circle of the negative, identifying negation with certain actors or possibilities that he glimpsed in the rebellion of the 1960s. His manifesto, *An Essay on Liberation,* is the faithful expression of that attempt. But this same gesture could be interpreted by critical negative thought as inconsistent with the imperative of negative thought. On the other extreme, Adorno wound up closed in by way of the abstract affirmation of his own negative capacity, strongly objecting to those very actors that Marcuse, in his moment, defended. The theoretical conflict facing negative thought can be evidenced from this difference between the two, when, on the one hand, negative thought affirms the emancipatory possibility of reality and of critical theory itself and, on the other hand, it announces, in an apocalyptic way, the universalized reification of reality, which ends up, in its totalitarian march, swallowing critical consciousness itself.

Negative thought and critical paranoia

In the light of some of the texts of Horkheimer and Adorno, it can be deduced that negative thought is not merely critical, but critical in a paranoid way.[14] The more flattering the criticism, the more it moves towards paralysis. It isn't strange, for example, to find medical metaphors in the exercise of negative thought, something like the messianic-paranoiac speeches which so repelled the very philosophers of the Frankfurt School, as illustrated in the following passage from Horkheimer's *Critique of Instrumental Reason:* "The disease of reason is that reason was born from man's urge to dominate nature, and the 'recovery' depends on insight into the nature of the original disease, not a cure of the latest symptoms."[15]

A clarifying observation appears in Martin Jay's meticulous historical reconstruction of the Frankfurt School. For the "founding fathers" of critical theory, the experience of German Nazism in the 1930s was so traumatic that consciousness subsequently could do no more than measure the degree of potential fascism in every contemporaneous form of social organization.[16] The problem here is that, carried to its extreme, negative thought bites its own tail, breaking the very link between social critique and political action insinuated as one of its promises. This is expressed in Horkheimer's and Adorno's mistrust regarding the expressions of radical politics in the 1960s, expressions that could well be interpreted (as Marcuse seemed to do, in his moment) as the crystallization of critical theory. As one of the leading chroniclers of the Frankfurt School, Martin Jay expresses it: "The desperate hopes of Horkheimer's wartime essay on the 'Authoritarian State' soon gave way to a deepening gloom about the chances for meaningful change . . . That imperative for praxis, so much a part of what some might call the Institut's heroic period, was no longer an integral part of its thought. Adorno's much quoted remark, made shortly before his death in 1969, that 'when I made my theoretical model, I could not have guessed that people would try to realize it with Molotov cocktails' . . . reflected instead a fundamental conclusion of the theory itself: negation could never be truly negated."[17]

This critical purism finds its most extensive expression in Adorno, in whom the critical-hermetic tendency seems exacerbated with the evolution of his thought. At the end of this evolution, he gives the impression that consciousness can do no more than take precautions, to dedicate itself to establishing a distance from all alienated consciousness, even at the price of solipsism: "If philosophy is still necessary," he proclaimed in 1962, "it is so only in the way it has been from time immemorial: as critique, as resistance to the expanding heteronymy."[18] Facing a world increasingly ruled by the law of reification, by the alienation of work and of power, by the spells of merchandise and of consumption, and by the authoritarianism of institutions, philosophy can do no more than be critical, and this in two senses: as refutation, irreconcilable with its object, and as a mode for situating said object as framed by the conditions that explain it and make it possible. Even as it is understood as an exercise of commitment to reality, philosophy winds up elevating itself above reality, like an aseptic entity that cannot mix itself with anything that might contaminate it: "Philosophy resigns by equating itself with what should in fact first be illuminated by philosophy."[19] Purified, exacerbated, or inverted Enlightenment? In the end, philosophy might seem to recognize that instrumental reason wins the battle inside Enlightenment, negating the only foundation for hope: namely, that in the Enlightenment project it was possible to turn back the dominant and dominating tendency of history.

*Some Scattered Connections between Negative Thought
and Latin America, To Be Taken, Depending on the
Occasion, with Enthusiasm, Caution, or Dismay*

The huge distance between Frankfurt and Latin America

The negative thought of the Frankfurt School found its favored fields for circulation among circuits of well-read intellectuals in the universities of industrialized countries (above all in Germany and in the U.S., where the School operated in distinct moments). It has scant diffusion in Spanish-speaking countries because it came to our countries by way of expensive publishers. It was in industrialized countries, above all in the 1960s and the beginnings of the 1970s, where the type of political processes, social mobilizations, forms of systemic rationalization and massive questioning of the status quo could find theoretical support in some strands of critical thought from Frankfurt.

But this empathy was ephemeral, given that negative thought evidenced, at its peak, an intrinsic difficulty with regard to formulating the proposals outlined in the preceding paragraphs. Owing to the state of development in this era in Latin America, the theoretical models most susceptible to being converted into platforms for social mobilization came from a less heterodox Marxism and from theories of dependency formulated from and towards Latin America, and from development discourse that had very little to do with the sensitivity of negative thought. Critical reflection within the region incorporated, at most, some considerations regarding the social impact of the culture industry and the manipulative power of mass communication media, whose analytical precedents were formulated by social scientists quite close to the spirit of the Frankfurt School. But they withdrew according to the political-ideological confrontations of the 1960s and 1970s, which in our region were lived in a particular manner. They did not take into account the principal connections that critical theory postulated in this regard, namely, the culture industry's full functionality for systemic rationalization.

The application of critical theory to social reflection in Latin America never constituted a significant theoretical project. It is nonetheless possible, today, for modern critical theory to weave a series of connections, demonstrated through practice itself, without the intention of proclaiming itself to be the heir of the Frankfurt School. The search for sociocultural spaces that can revive a will for collective emancipation persists as much in the industrialized world as in the Latin American periphery, but under new forms and with new actors. The tension between rationalization through technology and the market, on the one hand, and the will of collective subjects for proposing their autonomy with regard to this systemic logic, on the other hand, always finds new expressions (despite the apocalyptic outbursts of the late Adorno). Within these tensions, critical theory always offers concepts that can shed new light on contingency. The following paragraphs attempt such an exercise, aimed at an expanded perspective on some current social processes in Latin America.

Negative thought, crisis of exteriorization,
and loss of an emancipatory imagination

The glimmers of hope in negative thought dissolved when the implicit dialectic of exteriorization lost meaning. Industrial society made its contradictions evident and consistent, along with its subordination to instrumental reason, its contained and functional violence, its forms of repression and substitutes for freedom. Yet it didn't take its destiny into its own hands, nor did it seek mass emancipation. Exteriorization worked through one of its moments, namely, as the unmasking of domination; but it did not do so in its other moment of "the negation of appearance by being," as the overcoming of alienation, as the subversion of the repressive by the repressed.

In this way, theory was choked by its critique. Critical discourse has been updated in direct measure to its superfluity: contradictions were demonstrated, leaving no place for the noble effort of unmasking. As already indicated, nothing is more dismaying than criticism without emancipation. The problem stopped being the alienation of the spirit on the side of reality, and crystallized in the impotence of the spirit on the side of theory.

For Latin America, nonetheless, exteriorization had already been, almost from the onset, part of the very process of development. The real had always been exteriorized: it was seen in political violence, in military dictatorships, in cultural and ethnic discrimination, in misery and exclusion. In Latin America, "being" does not hide itself: it expresses itself as much in the repressed as in the repressor, in the integrated as in the excluded. Domination is and has always been public, visible, in an exteriorization that only connotes higher or more unpolished degrees of misery and of coercion, and never emancipation. Negative thought is inscribed in reality, almost as a stigma.

On the other hand, negation supposes, in its affirmative version, an act situated in an undetermined point in the future, by means of which a collective subject incarnates freedom and substantially changes the direction of history. In Latin America the referent for that moment of negation was, for a long time, a revolution self-defined as anti-capitalist and/or anti-imperialist. This revolution was thought, devised, and felt by those who assumed this moment of necessary negation as a point of inflection that would fill not just personal life, but the world, with meaning. In this manner the image of the revolution bestowed full coherence on personal activity (political, intellectual) insofar as the former worked towards that moment of mass emancipation. To work towards that instance of liberation, that irreducible event, was to bestow plenitude on life itself. Redemption and negation were a single thing under the threshold of revolution. The moment of the inversion of order—and not so much the subsequent order—was what mattered.

But that image, so seductive and so capable of inviting the sacrifice of one's own life and of generating an invisible but sublime tie among those who shared the image of revolution, was destroyed without being carried out, or relegated to minuscule groups and messianic delirium. The collapse of real socialism, the hard apprenticeship under the dictatorships, the crisis of paradigms in social theory, the defeat of Ortega in Nicaragua, the deterioration in Fidel's image in Cuba, and the most rudimentary analysis of correlated forces finished off the strength of this image (not of utopian order, but of utopian event). The intellectual was left without a committed science, the militant without a vital cause, the marginal, more alone than ever. And with the depleted dialectic, so dear to the Frankfurt School thinkers, the following questions arose, almost by way of afterthought: Is it possible to situate the affirmative moment of negation at another point and to preserve, within that moment, the capacity for mobilization, personal mysticism, the promise of freedom, the possibility of a fusion between personal action and mass irruption?

In the light of the death of these images and the oft-mentioned crises of development, of social articulation, and of alternatives: should we expect new roads for integration, ways to make being and appearance coincide, for producing a new form of societal synthesis, a new dialectic of exteriorization that negates alienation and affirms freedom, in a strong sense? Is it possible, in all, to think of a way committed to a movement negating structures which are dominant, exclusionary, manipulative? Or now, deprived of eventual revolutions and attractive models of development, is Latin America ready for its most lucid intellectuals to vindicate the closed version of negative thought, rejection-without-a-project, snubbing the very concept of projects?

The postmodern position also rejects all projects, although from a totally distinct perspective, which any Frankfurt School thinker would brand as reified thinking. What is certain is that the lack of confidence with regard to metanarratives doesn't begin with *The Postmodern Condition* by Lyotard,[20] but rather, at the very least, with the Dialectic of Enlightenment. While Adorno and Horkheimer question its implications, Lyotard and the postmoderns question its current validity. While critical theorists flow into a critical paranoia, the postmoderns turn it into ludic schizophrenia. The demystification that the critical theorists so often asked for arrives with postmodernity, but with such a degree of disintegration that no collective project would overcome the pulverizing effect that the new secularization would exercise over any discourse and project. Today, demystification does not guarantee freedom, but hurls itself into an extreme condition of contingency.

The place of criticism given the crises of intelligibility
and of articulation in social theory

As we have already suggested, the alluded loss of the utopian referent and of the horizon of communion between theory and practice, and between the individual and history, leaves the Latin American social sciences in a place of estrangement. As long as dependency theory had influence and currency, the images of development discourse or a possible revolution could be understood in a convincing articulation between the social sciences' idea of the socially intelligible on the one hand, and political activism's idea of social intervention on the other. Substantial changes in theoretical reflection, such as the waning of militant science, the fragmentation of knowledge that previously worked towards integration within a consistent whole, or the crisis of development discourse centered in planning and sustained modernization, undermined the "emancipatory mysticism" of the social scientist. Today's sacred words would have been sacrilegious during the years of big dreams: micro-project, interstice, small spaces, short term, low-profile, competitiveness.

On the one hand, casting doubt on the large-scale modernization projects that constituted the basic material of political-symbolic consumption at other moments in Latin America (whether in development discourse or in socialism) leads social scientists to question the place that their own knowledge production occupies within the orientation towards future social and political changes. On the other hand, the disenchantment and mistrust generated by the shattering of institutions, political failures, and social dismembering all lead to greater degrees of heterodoxy in the forms of apprehending reality. It currently turns out to be difficult to establish a limit between heterodoxy and eclecticism in the interpretive practice of the Latin American social scientist. Between the need to resort to tools from a very wide range of analytical perspectives, and the abandonment of globalizing categories that drew from strong ideologies, theory is exposed to the most hybrid formulations.

Totalization and synthesis lose their privileged place, not just within theory, but especially within the fusion of theory with politics, and of the intellectual with the masses. The field is freed, so that instrumental reason may uncoil itself freely through the spheres of social life. One could also think that the growing professionalization of the sociologist and of the political scientist in the present day, as well as a greater bias towards the pragmatic and technical in their theoretical practice, reflect this tendency. Criticism, as an intellectual function exercised from a socialist project — of individualism, selfishness, inequality of wealth, the production of goods, and political domination — now appears drastically cut back.[21] The questions can't be put off: How to exercise criticism from the perspective of social theory in Latin America today, in a meaningful way, and what contents might it establish, avoiding self-pitying pessimism or paralyzing fatalism? Is it possible to recover a mode of theory and practice in which criticism implies, in its turn, the potential for freeing features within social reality, the space for hopes oriented towards a more humanized order? Is it possible to promote a more affirmative, less heteronymous culture? Is it possible to socialize an ethic capable of "materializing" development? If this were the case: what are, even now, the signs emanating from the practice of the social scientist that portend new, creative forms of criticism in the sense just indicated? The following represents a first attempt to answer these questions.

New spaces and new approaches for exercising critical thought facing the fractures of modernization

New political, economic, and technological conditions make it increasingly difficult to imagine how particular projects will come together, uniting to transform society. On the one hand reality ratifies the suspicions of negative thought, given that in Latin America there is discrediting or widespread antipathy towards whatever "prescription" or recipe for emerging from the quagmire. But on the other hand, in this lack of a future, reason loses its possibilities for emancipatory articulation between the particular and the general.

Alternative proposals and/or perceptions nonetheless appear, which attempt, in a tentative and interstitial way, to negate the dominant paradigms of conventional modernization, without, on that account, becoming identified with the status quo dictated by the march of the market. Some of the values emerging in such perceptions merit a fuller, more exhaustive explanation.

First, the valorization of democracy as an order in which conflicts are resolved through dialogue, negotiation, and consensus, and as a necessary context for the least coercive possible articulations between the State and civil society, in ways that privilege communicational rationality. Democracy is also valorized as a political foundation for the reconciliation of conflicts such as those between the technical versus political dimensions of development, between planning and the market, between the local and the national. Finally, democracy is valorized as a spring for social participation, the decentralization of decisions, and creating a culture of citizenship. It's no mere chance that some Latin American political scientists, occupied with reflecting on the processes of re-democratization in our countries, today incorporate into their interpretive baggage the theory of communicative action elaborated by Habermas, the last great paladin of Frankfurt. The concern with communicative transparency (in the rationality of dialogue through the unfolding of a democratic order, and in its articulation with political logic and with the use of public space) has important theoretical precedents in the tradition of critical theory (especially in the renovation of critical theory via Habermas).

Second, the revalorization of social movements and of the social fabric, and, in the same sense, the revalorization of civil society as "polymorphous" in facing the State's homogenizing action. The State, in its turn, responds to the will of a few, conceiving new forms of doing politics, which would be less subject to the interference of party politics or the practices of specific clients, and more centered in the cultural determinations of its actors. The so-called new social movements (or grassroots, base groups, or popular organizations) acquire special emphasis in this sense. For their marginal or interstitial space within society and with regard to the State and the market, they can materialize "counter-hegemonic" logics where solidarity, resistance, cooperativism, autonomy and/or collective participation predominate. From there, social energies stretch outwards, without being absorbed by instrumental reason by the politics of co-optation from the political system, or by mercantile logic. It isn't easy to ponder the degree and extensiveness of this phenomenon, or to what measure it tends to turn into an idealized construction for social scientists seeking new actors for new utopias. But beyond this spurious condition, which is always present and is best taken as a given, the rescue of the "counterhegemonic" flows of the social movements (eventually subject to new logics, not submitted to systemic rationalization) likewise resonates in critical theory. One could similarly evoke Marcuse's rescue of the countercultural movements of the 1960s, as well as Habermas' more recent defense of worlds of life, facing systemic reason. If in those social movements everyday life counts for more and the electoral battle for less, and if the strength of the territorial-neighborhood dimension is greater than that of the political-institutional insertion, and if the weight of symbolic-cultural vindication equals that of material demands, then they constitute themselves as small "promises of emancipation" in the eyes of critical theory.

These perceptions embody a vision of reality which is critical, but not fatalistic: the rescue of the new social movements demonstrates a concern lest the constitution of collective identities fall into the stigma of reifying social actors. To prefer social movements as opposed to the traditional political parties is to privilege logics which are less instrumental forms of political practice, and more autonomous with regard to the social dynamic. The revalorization of democracy in a broad, deep sense further implies the intent to mold a democratic culture, and not just a majority-elected government—that is, an ideal of citizenship inscribed in the constructive discourse of Enlightenment.

Alternative forms of sociability, processing demands and horizontal communication, would bestow increasing value on these spaces. There, they might start constituting new central points for critical humanists who are sailing along, bereft of large-scale narratives, adrift in a sea of post-ideological disenchantment. The democratization of society could become a new version of some historical ideals of critical thought: progressive de-hierarchization of the relations between distinct social actors across the field of the economy of solidarity and of new social movements; a growing cultural pluralism that is opposed to the exclusivist slant that modernizing rationality imposes with respect to endogenous cultures; and a growing communicative fluidity oriented towards democratizing the processing of demands in public space, towards converting the excluded into new "communicating subjects" within this public space.

In this new perspective, the exercise of criticism is grouped into a series of functions difficult to order hierarchically. On one hand, the exercise of criticism is fleshed out as the denunciation of totalitarian danger in traditional sociological and sociopolitical interpretation of the subjects. From this trench for criticism appears the censure of the functionalist and developmentalist tradition, for example, and of social subjectivity's submission to quantifiable and comparable terms. The censure argues that such submission redounds in the manipulation of social actors from a force that tries to situate itself on top of them (call this force the State, the party, social or intellectual science). There is a censuring of the Marxist tradition, on the other hand, in its tendency to construct social subjects by way of their "structural" determinants, reducing the specificity of some to the generality of others. There's an objection, as well, to Marxism's historical tendency to impel a kind of social change with visions of deterministic and closed worlds. The criticism that followers of Nietzsche, Heidegger, and the Frankfurt School have made, from different perspectives, of the primacy of modern ratio (commensurating reason, which on account of being constrictive-constructive, is very exclusivizing) is applied with special force to the Latin American left and to the normative planner. That criticism is applied to the left because it fell into the temptation of judging, measuring, and reducing everything according to the canon of its own ideology. That criticism is applied to the planner for having fallen into the illusion that social reality was intrinsically measurable, rationalizable, and directible from a so-called science of development. (This idea is developed at greater length, in this text, in the chapter entitled "Is the Social Think-able without Metanarratives?")

Another field from which to exercise criticism, with important theoretical referents in the tradition of critical theory, is that of the culture industry. Within this frame it is argued that the ceaseless tensions between cultural identity and modernity could be resolved with integrative effects through the new communicative potential of the culture industry. The effective deployment of the culture industry nonetheless can also take on more conflictive indications, owing to high levels of social disintegration, segmented access, and to the close link between the culture industry and transnational economic power. Because the impact of communicative and informative globalization on endogenous cultures is uncertain, critical consciousness has a key role to play in this area of our societies. The culture industry, and within it, the information industry, penetrate the collective imagination in a systematic, everyday manner. Its power over personal subjectivity is thus seen as facilitated by the spontaneous tendency towards the a-critical acceptance of its messages. As a spokesperson for negative thought might express it, the culture industry and the power of information are embodied forms of dominant ideology and institutionalized practices of systemic rationalization: it is in this manner that the dominant culture invisibly but effectively penetrates the skin of all the other cultures. The invisible and systemic nature of its manipulation merits the application of critical unmasking. So much the better if behind every unwary television watcher there were a Frankfurtian Superego, warning against the possibly alienating effects of the culture industry.

The exercise of criticism consists, then, in unmasking the reductive rationalities of the models of knowledge and the predominant forms of culturization and social action. These rationalities and forms are, by their very reductiveness and predominance, alienating, dehumanizing, and all the negative epithets that one might conceive from within the trench of critical humanism. The criticism of dominant rationalities is diversified in various criticisms: instrumental or manipulative rationality, economic or economist rationality, "professionalized" rationality of power, and the ethnocentric biases in the rationality of progress.

That this form of criticism has its precedents in the critical theory of the Frankfurt School becomes even more evident in touching on the oft-mentioned concept of alienation. The wealth — or indeterminacy? — of this concept proves advantageous, given its significance in the field of culture, sociology, politics, and psychopathology. It is advantageous that the concept of alienation, according to its uses, leads to another series of neighboring concepts frequently appearing in criticism of the rationalities of domination: reification, instrumentalization, domination, coercion, manipulation, co-optation, denaturalization, passivity, inauthenticity, etc. All of them clearly carry a negative connotation.

Finally, these critical approaches seem to share a metavalue repeated throughout its scattered discourses, that could be defined as the option for an exhaustively democratic order, with "exhaustive" indicating that the relations susceptible to being democratized aren't just those that mediate between the State and civil society, but between all kinds of institutions (families, municipalities, schools, workplaces, public institutions, and services), and in the most varied planes (the political, social, cultural, economic, and technological). In this context, the expansion of critical consciousness appears as a phenomenon multiplying across all the spaces of social interaction, from the familiar to the political, from the plane of personal communication to that of public action, and from the field of culture to that of economy. It shouldn't seem strange, then, that in the epistemological opinion of those who share this metavalue of exhaustive democratization, interdisciplinarity and participative research would also appear as favored practices.

*"Another Development" and the critique of instrumental
reason and of Enlightenment reason in Latin America*

The instrumentalist model attributed to the prevailing modernization in Latin America has been questioned from the entrenched heterodoxy of alternative discourse known as "Another Development."[22] This critique comes from social scientists situated outside of the sphere of the state. Many of them are closely involved with NGOs (non-governmental organizations) engaged in research and activism, dedicated to study and to promoting communitarian forms of social organization, appropriate technologies, participative social politics, organic relations with the surrounding environment, the expansion of popular culture, respect for autochthonous identities, and/or greater attention to local phenomena and grassroots groups. These social scientists argue that the dominant development model (initially, a discourse of encouraging development or nationalization, which subsequently gave way to the neoliberal model) neglects the qualitative dimension of social life, sidesteps endogenous expressions and ethnic and regional identities, and tends to emulate models of development of industrialized societies which exercise a disastrous effect on the environment. In contrast with this, the paladins of Another Development welcome experiences which are communitarian, autochthonous, participatory, and that undo the hierarchies involved in promoting development. They privilege development which is social, cultural, and local over that which is economic, technological, and national. The relativization of instrumental reason leads to standing apart from the terrain of the great conflicts of central power, limiting itself to minimal spaces of social interaction, where it seems more viable "to purge" relations of their propensity to manipulation.

The critical social scientist's preoccupation with new social movements, countercultural initiatives, ethnic minorities, experiences of communitarian development, and small scale projects demonstrates that the critical function does not close itself off in pure negativity. Negativity, as the moment of rejecting the dominant logic (as manipulative, instrumental, coercive), seeks its positive complement in small actors within the social fabric. That's where the researcher dedicated to an unconventional kind of research (call it action-research or participant-research) wants to encounter instances of alterity with regard to the system. Negation's affirmative instance then appears not as tomorrow's generalized utopia but as today's everyday, in-between reality. This is the reality of shantytown dwellers building their own housing, of community soup kitchens, backyard vegetable gardens, agricultural communes, self-managed workshops, programs for adult education, popular medicine, the defense of nature, and many others. There, the instrumental is submitted to an ethical principal, not made explicit, but which the researcher unravels (or imagines?) over the course of these small-scale practices. It's nonetheless worth questioning the degree of mystification incurred when the paladins of Another Development defend these interstitial experiences. That is, do counter-hegemonic logics (of solidarity, anti-hierarchical, participatory) really extend, day by day, throughout the social fabric? Or is that mystification an expression of the researcher's own desire and urgent need to construct a new social actor with emancipatory potential? It's worth asking, maybe even more suspiciously, if it is possible to design and construct a distinct societal order departing from the multiplication of those interstices all the way across society.

But despite these reservations, various elements draw this new current of social scientists, set on a critical intellectual project, into association with critical theory of the Frankfurt school:

They begin by exposing to critical artillery the very practice of knowledge production, and by this route they question their own place as social researchers. The wager for new modes of understanding research (as action or participation) effectively reflects an effort to adopt, in their own experience, the challenge of criticism, without implying an "Adorno-like" withdrawal from the worldly din.

There exists a determination to recover the ideal of the social scientist as engaged in processes of emancipatory social transformation, and to locate theoretical practice in that direction, precisely by means of an effective proximity between the researcher and the actors whom that researcher regards as agents for change. That proximity can be achieved by way of what's been described as action-research or participant-research.

In this emerging production of knowledge and new perception, negation has two parts: critique of the totality (of the general order) and the affirmation of what denies the totality (the interstitial, the peripheral). One might nonetheless object that no dialectical relation exists between the two parts of the negation: dominant reason is not seen as overcome or freed by the sparks flying from the interstices. Rather, the "emancipatory-in-between" coexists with the "coercive-general," neither abolishing it or coming to dispute its hegemony.

In this way, negation does not free itself from the negated, that is, from the general order. Rather, it only recognizes spaces in which that order is resisted. From this perspective, there is no absolute co-optation on the part of dominant reason. Neither is there a process of transcending said reason on the part of contrahegemonic logics, always confined to microspaces.[23] So is this critical function of social knowledge situated in the middle of the road, between the more optimistic Marcuse and the more pessimistic Adorno: the counter-hegemonic does not expand to the point of producing a generalized emancipatory movement, nor is there a total closure of the world from the dominant order. The theoretical referent most adjusted to this perspective could be found today in Michel Foucault's celebrated theory of power, according to which the discourses of power and its distinct forms of rationalization ceaselessly generate discourses and forms of resistance on the part of the subjected, without this tension between powers and resistance's taking on a necessarily dialectical solution, through which the logics of resistance accede to power.

In conclusion: Common leitmotivs in critical theory and in critical social research in Latin America

Passing over distances, objects of study, modes of insertion in the production of social knowledge and intellectual strategy, points of affinity exist between critical theory and the emerging tendencies of Latin American social research. Both cases engage in a constant exercise of interpretation that "denounces" reality, which seeks to unveil the operation of dominant rationalities (formal, instrumental, co-active, commodity fetishism) within distinct boundaries: in the statist exercise of power, in the family structure, in educational institutions, in culture and in everyday life. In both cases the notion of alienation is used, in its diverse meanings, to mark the distance between the general order and that which negates it. In both cases there exists a certain passion for social rationality, and the implicit or explicit conviction that the social possibilities of emancipation or of closure are played out on the plane of that rationality. In both cases there exists an almost Manichaean vision of politics, or at least of the current forms of politics, understanding that this is, above all, a field of domination and of alienation, and that institutionalized politics "taints" the one who performs it. In both cases, the social functions that theory desires for itself are the critique of the hegemonic order and the recognition of subjects and practices with emancipatory signs. This would deal with utilizing theory towards the dissemination of critical consciousness and of knowledge that would permit greater comprehension and autonomy for social actors with "emancipatory potential." It would also deal with restoring and consecrating those actors and social practices that eventually bear counter-hegemonic logic.

It is also clear that there are important differences between the critical theory of the Frankfurt School and the critical social research emerging in Latin America. The thinkers of Frankfurt, parodying an expression of Kafka, could brand the preoccupation and rescue of interstices and small logic, so very characteristic of Latin American alternative thought, as one more knot in the master's whip. And Adorno's purity could be ironized in turn from the "social cauldron" of Latin America, where misery's extension and profound intercultural crossbreeding constitute an opaque wall against which the subtleties of criticism shatter into fragments.

But it is not my intention to spin too fine a thread in this sense. Instead, I am only trying to provide an overview of the terrain so that Latin American critical reflection can recover something positive from negative thought and the critical theory of Frankfurt. Even if it's only to stir up the fire and from there, to venture new wagers.

Notes

1 Especially T. W. Adorno and Max Horkheimer, and, in some moments, the thought of Herbert Marcuse, for example his criticisms of Soviet socialism and the alienation of labor in *The One-Dimensional Man: Studies in the Ideology of Advanced Industrial Society* (Boston: Beacon Press, 1964).

2 Herbert Marcuse, *Reason and Revolution: Hegel and the Rise of Social Theory* (Boston: Beacon, 1960), ix.

3 Max Horkheimer, "On the Concept of Philosophy," *Eclipse of Reason* (New York: Seabury, 1974), 182.

4 Horkheimer, "On the Concept of Philosophy," 183.

5 T. W. Adorno, "Cultural Criticism and Society," *Prisms* 29 (London: Neville Spearman, 1967).

6 While the limits that separate both concepts — critical theory and negative thought — aren't totally clear, in the following pages negative thought is associated with the more closed version of critical theory, which, in Adorno and Horkheimer especially, leaves less and less space for an affirmative moment in reflection.

7 Marcuse, *Reason and Revolution,* (Boston: Beacon, 1960), ix.

8 Marcuse, *Reason and Revolution,* (Boston: Beacon, 1960), 312.

9 Marcuse, *An Essay on Liberation* (Boston: Beacon, 1969).

10 Marcuse, "Supplementary Epilogue," *Reason and Revolution* (New York: Humanities Press, 1954), 401.

11 Qtd. in Castellet, *Lectura de Marcuse* (Barcelona: Seix Barral, 1971), 48.

12 Adorno and Horkheimer, "The Concept of Enlightenment" in *The Dialectic of Enlightenment,* trans. John Cumming (New York: Herder and Herder, 1972), 24.

13 Herbert Marcuse, *Etica y revolución,* trans. Aurelio Alvarez (Madrid: Taurus, 1979), 146.

14 For example, in Horkheimer, *A Critique of Instrumental Reason,* modernity assumes the figure of an airplane without a pilot that blindly falls. In *The Jargon of Authenticity* (Evanston, Ill., Northwestern University Press, 1973), Adorno interprets the philosophy of Heidegger discovering "semantic traps" on all sides. Even in the extensively celebrated concept of repressive desublimation in Marcuse, there is no advance in freedom that is exempt from degenerating into a new mask of repression.

15 Horkheimer, "On the Concept of Philosophy," 176.

16 "Thus, for example, the Frankfurt School's critique of American society sometimes

appeared to suggest that no real distinction existed between Nazi coercion and 'the culture [or critical] industry.' In fact, so some of its critics would charge, the Nazi experience had been so traumatic for the Institut's members that they could judge American society only in terms of its Fascist potential" (Martin Jay, *The Dialectical Imagination: A History of the Frankfurt School and the Institute for Social Research, 1923– 1950,* [Boston: Little Brown, 1973], 297).

17 Jay, *The Dialectical Imagination*, 256, 279.

18 In Adorno, "Why Still Philosophy," a radio conference transmitted originally in 1962 in Germany. See the compilation *Critical Models: Interventions and Catchwords* (New York: Columbia University Press, 1998).

19 Adorno, "Why Still Philosophy?" in *Critical Models*, 11. If Adorno is referring here to the dangers of positivism, it suffices to consider his final texts and interventions aimed at extending it to all thought which is committed to and identified with situational positions.

20 Jean-Francois Lyotard, *The Postmodern Condition* (Minneapolis: University of Minnesota Press, 1984).

21 According to Agnes Heller's perspective, synthetic and clear for these pages' aims, socialist criticism can be divided into four groups of objectives: selfishness, individualism, and a lifestyle based on oppression; inequality in wealth, the production of goods; and political domination. In correlation, the emancipatory model then supposes the following characteristics: new forms of life based on immediacy, community, direct democracy, the elimination of the division of labor; the provision or abolition of property, elimination of poverty, control of the assignation of goods and services; the abolition of the State and of the division of labor, the end of fetishism and manipulation, the free development of personal capacities; and the abolition of the State and all political institutions — that is, the centralization of power — or the restriction of individual freedom by way of self-restriction. (See Agnes Heller and Ferenc Feher, *Anatomía de la izquierda occidental [Anatomy of the Western Left]*, Spanish translation by M. A. Galmarini of the original, unpublished English version [Barcelona: Ediciones Península], 46–47).

22 See, for example, Fernando Henrique Cardoso, et al. *Another Development: Approaches and Strategies.* Ed. Marc Nerfin. (Uppsala: Dag Hammarskold Foundation, 1977) and Manfred A. Max-Neef, *Human Scale Development: conception, application, and further reflections;* with contributions from Antonio Elizalde, Martín Hopenhayn; foreword by Sven Hamrell (New York: Apex Press, 1991).

23 Starting from the contributions of this current critique, it isn't easy to reconstruct a universal model that breaks with the negative moment of criticism. Rather, there are many dispersed forces, with multiple meanings, involving, among other things, the impact of the sensitivity of other social scientists and politicians, and proposals for projects, self-managed and going in multiple directions.

6 ❄ Postmodernism and Neoliberalism in Latin America

The debate about postmodernism has, at its extremes, two opposite positions: on the one hand, that of "postmodern enthusiasts," who proclaim the collapse of modernity, of its cultural bases, and of its paradigms in the social sciences, politics, art, and philosophy; on the other hand, the position of the "critical modernists," who recognize the crisis of modernity as a point of inflection that does not suppose the obsolescence of modernity, but rather forms part of its inherent dynamic. From this perspective, postmodernism is no more than modernity reflecting on itself and explaining its unresolved conflicts.[1]

The critical modernists see in the postmodern enthusiasts an intellectual fad of the decade of the eighties, which, like all fads, is marked by frivolity and inconsistency. The postmodern enthusiasts, on the other hand, see in the idea of the crisis of modernity the reflection of a wide range of political, intellectual, and cultural phenomena that transcend the academic field and permeate the sensibility of the people, daily life, and models of communication.[2] In the following pages, we will situate ourselves in an intermediate position, one of "criticism without renunciation" of modernity, but conceding to the postmodernism debate a series of political and cultural implications that prevent us from simply dismissing it pejoratively as an intellectual fad. What I intend is to incorporate the postmodern perspective in order to enrich or recreate postponed challenges within modernity itself. I will summarize the positions of postmodernism in a schematic manner, emphasizing its ideological ambivalence and its differences from the paradigms and options of modernity. Then, I will attempt to survey the challenges that postmodernism poses in Latin America in particular by shifting the emphasis from the so-called crisis of modernity to the equally important question of the crisis of *styles* of modernization, which will lead me to consider the connections between postmodernism and the current influence of neoliberalism in Latin America.

In Lyotard's well-known definition, postmodernism is the crisis of metanarratives. Metanarratives are understood as the transcendental categories that modernity has invented in order to interpret and normalize reality. These categories — such as the advancement of reason, the emancipation of man, progressive self-knowledge, and the freedom of the will — spring from the project of the Enlightenment and function to integrate, in an articulated direction, the process of the accumulation of knowledge and the development of the productive forces and of sociopolitical consensus and control. They all refer, in turn, to an idealization of the idea of progress — that is, the conviction that history marches in a determined direction in which the future is, by definition, an improvement on the present. The metanarratives constitute the cognitive parameters that determine intelligible, rational, and predictable reality. Perceptive thought consists of using the faculties of reason to get to the bottom of phenomena — be they of nature, of history, or of society — in order to be able to predict their behavior "rationally." In this way, the metanarratives authorize us to describe and normalize; they show us how things are, where they should lead to, and how to resolve the gap between what is and what should be. In this sense, both classical liberalism and Marxism are inspired by a shared, Enlightenment origin, invoking universal principles that have, for a long time, exhibited enormous mobilizing capacity.

The postmodernists question the force of the metanarratives of modernity. They point out that such axiomatic categories have lost explanatory capacity and legitimizing force. They associate this obsolescence with diverse causes, among which the following stand out: the revolution of paradigms in the exact and natural sciences and its subsequent impact on the social sciences; the acceleration of technological change and the consequent diversification of processes and products, which prevents the perception of society as homogeneous and extended unities and imposes increasingly higher degrees of complexity, movement, and flexibility on it; the microcomputer revolution, and the resulting diffusion of data processing, which brings a proliferation of signs and languages that pulverizes the single model of rationality (our situation becomes interpretable from many possible perspectives, according to the software we use to deal with different problems we confront); the loss of the centrality of the subject in a historical period in which the complexity of cultural structures and fragmentation makes the idea of a generic human identity — necessary for projects of human emancipation, collective self-consciousness, or any global utopia — inconceivable; the depersonalization of knowledge through its conversion into the strategic input of new productive processes, and the multiplication of information to totally unmeasurable levels, which impedes preserving the idea of the subject as the "bearer" of knowledge and makes any ideology that pretends to integrate available knowledge into a comprehensive interpretation of the world impossible; and finally, the "communicative ecstasy" (Baudrillard) caused by the combined effects of data processing, capital flows, and telecommunications, by virtue of which national frontiers and regional identities are dissolving under the dizzying pace of communication.

The discourse of the postmodern situates itself in a position of consummated facts. It does not present itself as an attempt to demystify modernity but rather as an ex post facto verification of the fact that modernity has already lost its mystique. The postmodernists, at least explicitly, do not pretend to precipitate the entropy of the concepts and visions that govern modernity, such as the rationality of history, progress, and integration via the homogenization of values. Rather, they claim to recognize this entropy in the condition of the present. Nevertheless, for those who have followed the debate, it is not clear whether this crisis and decline of the metanarratives of modernity is merely being described or whether it is being provoked "from outside" by the postmodern enthusiasts themselves.[3] This ambiguity comes out of the contingent ideological functions that postmodern discourse tends to assume, which we will examine later on.

The principal targets of postmodern discourse are, in summary:

— The idea of progress. For the postmodernists, history does not march in an ascending path; it is discontinuous, asynchronic, pregnant with multiple directions and with growing margins of uncertainty about the future. There is no internal and specific rationality that regulates the movement of history but, rather, multiple, incongruous forces that give results that are unexpected, provisional, partial, and dispersed.[4]

— The idea of a vanguard. Since there is no single rationality or directionality to history, even less recognizable and legitimate is the aspiration of a group that appropriates for itself the rational interpretation of history and that deduces a normative directionality on a global scale based on this interpretation. Whether in politics, science, art, or culture, and whether the vanguard is the party, the state, the educational elite, or an aesthetic movement, no one can claim to constitute the group chosen or destined to establish totalizing orientations. Once the category of the directionality and rationality of history is questioned, all vanguards seem to be invested with authoritarian and discretionary power.[5]

— The idea of modernizing integration or of integrating modernization.[6] According to the criteria of modernization, being in step with the times involves increasing productivity, developing ever-higher levels of formal education in the population, and incorporating an enlightened sensibility into the masses. This is rejected by the postmoderns. The Enlightenment and the industrial utopias that are the basis of modernity and that permit the understanding of development as a progressive process of homogenization are put into doubt by ascribing to them an excess of normativity, an ethnocentric bias and a pretension to cultural cohesion that proves anachronistic in light of the "proliferation of variety" of the "new times."

— Ideologies. To the preceding is added, for good measure, the disqualification of all ideology, understood as an integrated vision of the world that allows one to explain a great diversity of phenomena from a few basic principles, or from which a desired image of order, considered universally valid, can be projected. The disqualification of ideologies automatically brings with it the disqualification of utopias, understood as images of an ideal social order that possess an orienting force for decision making in the present and that provide a unified directionality toward the future. If utopian thought has been considered, from Renaissance humanism to modernism, as an exercise of the freedom of spirit, in postmodernity it seems more like an authoritarian ruse.[7]

If the "postmodern narrative" declares the obsolescence of the idea of progress, historical reason, vanguards, integrating modernization, and ideologies and utopias, what is it that it proclaims in exchange? Basically, the exaltation of diversity, aesthetic and cultural individualism, multiplicity of languages, forms of expression and life-projects, and axiological relativism. The vagueness of this proposal does not disturb its supporters, since it fits in perfectly with the idea of the indeterminacy of the future, which, according to them, sets the tone of the times.

In these general orientations, the postmodern narrative borrows from multiple disciplinary sources. From anthropology and ethnology it takes cultural relativism and the critique of ethnocentrism. From philosophy it takes the critique of humanism and of the centrality of the (universal/ particular, free/conscious) subject, and from semiotics the primacy of structures and signs over subjects. From antipsychiatry and the "radical" variants of psychoanalysis it takes the exaltation of polymorphous desire and the critique of "philogenetic reductionism." From political theory it takes the idea that society is composed of an inextricable interweaving of micropowers and "local," rather than universal, power games. From aesthetics it takes the taste for combining heterogeneous and asynchronic styles (the classical and the romantic, the baroque and the functionalist, the rococo and the futurist). And from sociology it takes the recognition of the heterogeneity and complexity of social dynamics.

All of this might lead one to think that postmodern discourse is a sane antidote to the excessively ethnocentric, rationalist, and mechanist tendencies of modern society. If that is the case, postmodernism could be thought of as an internal movement of modernity itself, a critique modernity puts into effect in order to exorcise its entropy. But, in fact, postmodernism frequently acquires very different pretensions and functions: In effect, it transforms itself into an ideology, disguising its normative judgments as descriptions, and ends up seeing what it wants to see.

The ideologization of postmodern discourse may be glimpsed when one focuses on the service that it lends to the political-cultural offensive of the market economy. Neoliberalism has profitably capitalized on postmodernist rhetoric in order to update its longed-for project of cultural hegemony. This project, the dream of liberalism in its formative stages, was frustrated by the universalist ethic of modern humanism, by political mobilization, and by social pressures. What many neoliberals saw, especially in industrialized countries, is the possibility that reculturization, via a seductive postmodern narrative, could serve to legitimize the market offensive of the eighties—in other words, could make the desires of the public coincide with the promotion of pro-market policies and with the consolidation of a transnational capitalist system. It is no accident that elements of what we are calling the postmodern narrative have been disseminated, at least in good measure, by neoliberals and disenchanted leftists seduced by anarcho-capitalism.[8] What are the connections between postmodern critiques and the project of neoliberal cultural hegemony? The exaltation of diversity leads to the exaltation of the market, considered as the only social institution that orders without coercion, guaranteeing a diversity of tastes, projects, languages, and strategies. Only by expanding the reach of the market can the interventionist and globalizing excesses of the state be avoided. The state itself should be restricted to subsidiary functions in places where the market shows itself to be insufficient. Economic deregulation and privatization appear as almost ad hoc policies for the full realization of the "ludic individualism" heralded by postmodern discourse. Deregulation is the correlative in the practical sphere of the theoretical celebration of diversity. In the face of this wager, in which everything is potentially permissible, problems of social disparity, structural heterogeneity, insufficient development, and the like lose relevance.[9]

The critique of the vanguards translates into: a critique of the transformational function of politics, unless the transformation is in the direction of privatization and deregulation (anarcho-capitalism);[10] and a critique of state planning and intervention in the organization, regulation, and direction of the economy (by reducing the state to the status of one social actor among others, in order to then object to its interventionism as involving the will to domination of one actor over the rest).

Without an emancipatory dynamic that runs beneath events or that guides the actions of humanity, nothing permits the questioning of consumer society, waste, the alienation of work, the growing split between the industrialized and developing countries, social marginality, technocracy, or the way in which productive forces are misused.

The critique of ideologies culminates, in particular, in a criticism of Marxism and its humanist-socialist variants; the critique of utopias tends to focus in particular on egalitarian utopias or on any ideal that proposes, as a task of the present, the redistribution of social wealth and power.

The critique of modernizing integration transforms structural heterogeneity into a healthy example of diversity and relativizes conventional indicators of development, such as expanded and improved services in the fields of health and education.

The synchrony between the market offensive and a cofunctional postmodernist cultural sensitizing is noteworthy. It is here that our analysis requires precision. The defense of a status quo governed by unequal competition, social inequality, the will of the transnationals, and the discretionary self-policing of finance capital cannot be automatically deduced from the verification of the crisis of the models of modernity. The discursive astuteness of postmodern neoliberalism resides in its effective articulation of euphemisms, which the interests of the centers of political and economic power, and of sectors identified with the "free" economy, can use to cover themselves with an aesthetic aura that undoubtedly makes them more seductive. It is more attractive to talk about diversity than the market, about desire than the maximization of profits, about play than conflict, about personal creativity than the private appropriation of economic surplus, about global communication and interaction than the strategies of transnational companies to promote their goods and services. It is more seductive to speak in favor of autonomy than against planning, or in favor of the individual than against the state (and against public expenditure and social welfare policies). In this way, the social contradictions of capitalism, accentuated on the Latin American periphery, disappear behind the exaltation of forms and languages. The economic crisis — the worst we have experienced in this century — is hidden under the euphemism of a beautiful anarchy, and structural heterogeneity is converted into the creative combination of the modern and the archaic, "our" peripheral incarnation and anticipation of the postmodern.

The above suggests some of the ways in which postmodernism can be used to produce a "strategic" package of euphemisms that dress up the neoliberal project of cultural hegemony, which is the ideological correlative of the transnational offensive, in a way that penetrates the sensibility of the public. It does this, basically, by opposing an aesthetic fascination with chaos with an ethical concern with development. Negligence of the future assumes the appealing figure of a passion for the present. The postmodern narrative, however, is susceptible to many interpretations and uses. It cannot be reduced to the market offensive and to the ideological uses that some neoliberal strategies make of it.[11] This is so for a number of reasons. In the first place, many enthusiasts of the postmodern narrative are politically situated at a considerable distance from neoliberal positions.[12] In the second place, positions such as the passion for the present, aestheticism, the exaltation of diversity, the rejection of ethnocentrism, the desire for open societies, the return to pluralist individualism, cultural polymorphism, and the prioritization of creativity can be adapted to political projects of another kind. In the third place, the questioning of cultural paradigms and matrices, in light of emerging scenarios, does not necessarily lead to the defense of anarcho-capitalism. Finally, the critique of paradigms that have directed the styles of modernization and develpment has also generated alternative proposals and/or visions that, far from uniting with the deregulating offensive of the market, seek to mobilize social creativity in totally different directions. The following considerations, oriented to Latin American reality, may be indicative of such directions.

The industrial model, centered in the substitution of imports, was discovered to have less integrating capacity than was supposed at its beginning, as much in terms of its internal insufficiencies as of exogenous variables (the heritage of Catholicism, etc.). The model also produced destructive, collateral effects, especially by imposing an imitative pattern in which, in the name of modernization, questions of cultural identity and ecological preservation were relinquished to sectors that incorporated the values and expectations of industrial culture, at the same time leaving other sectors in a position of frustrated expectations, condemned to social marginality and economic informality by the same model of development that saw the desired benefits of growth pass them by. The insufficiencies or trade-offs of this model do not, however, have to impel us towards a neoliberal alternative. The dynamic insufficiencies of accumulation, noted by the Economic Commission on Latin America (CEPAL) for a long time, and the process of economic growth without social equity, which has characterized our countries even in times of relative consensus regarding the modernization paradigm, do not find a remedy in the neoliberal prescriptions. On the contrary, such prescriptions sharpen the regressive tendencies in matters of social integration and balanced growth instead of blunting them. Finally, neoliberalism massively promotes imitative patterns of consumption that have very little to do with the exaltation of diversity and the criticism of ethnocentrism. To promote, in particular, a diversity in the consumption of goods and services may well be a form of promoting, in general, a specific, and implacable, economic logic.

The styles of modernization in Latin America have shown an excessive privilege for instrumental rationality over substantive rationality. Consequently, they have delegated instrumental knowledge and power to elites who have not acquired representative legitimacy and who have often tended towards technocracy. The predominance of technical reason has frequently resulted in the sacrifice of social participation in decisions and measures, and in a democracy restricted by the power of "expertise." Curiously, the uncritical exaltation that postmodern neoliberals make of the new technologies does not reverse this tendency but rather celebrates it, under the pretext that the new technologies are "spontaneously" decentralized. Faced with a similar "technologist" triumphalism, the warnings of the Frankfurt school to the effect that the crisis of modernity does not have its cause in a supposed entropy of substantive rationality or of collective utopias, but rather in the growing predominance of instrumental reason over the values and utopias characteristic of humanism, acquire full force in Latin America.[13] The nature of the corporate interests involved in the deregulation of the acceleration of technological change and the productivist euphoria that accompanies it does not annul but rather confirms these "modern" suspicions.

It is essential to examine the role of the state in Latin American societies in more than one aspect. In the economic aspect, the centrality of the state in stimulating development has entered into a crisis of effectiveness. It is not necessary to be neoliberal to object to state hypertrophy, the gigantism of the public sector, or the rigidity of the bureaucracies. In the political aspect, the examination of the state's role is related to the new vitality of the theme of democracy, its principles, and its most appropriate forms. The emphasis on social agreement, citizen participation, decentralization, civil society, and autonomy on a local or regional scale aims to minimize the coercive effects of the state and to increase its social legitimacy as an articulator of different social actors.

All of the above does not suppose the alternative of laissez-faire, however. The market has not proven to be the most efficient mechanism of decentralization, democratic participation, and autonomy. Undoubtedly, the market has made important contributions to economic dynamism under certain circumstances and in some countries. But frequently, it has required the help of authoritarian and repressive governments to avoid the conflicts generated by its discriminatory effects in matters of access to goods and services.

It is important to reconsider the role of planning in the economic and social ordering and directionality imposed by development. This supposes the critique of normative planning, the incorporation of new perceptual inputs in the exercise of the planner, the revision of the dominant rationalities sedimented in the practice of planning, and a greater coherence in articulation between the technical and political dimensions in the decision processes.[14] These critiques and revisions, however, do not force the renunciation of planning nor the reduction of it to its minimal expression. Nor do they suppose that all planning is the negation of diversity, the predominance of a technocratic caste, or the inhibition of autonomy. Planning is opposed to the negligence of the future,[15] but it does not have to sacrifice passion for the present. This future directionality can, provided it finds its appropriate forms of application, give meaning to the present. It is not a question of doing away with planning but of designing it in new ways to meet the challenges of postmodernity.

In tandem with the previous point, the critique of the directionality of our present history does not have to be confused with the rejection of all directionality. What is in question are the styles of linear development that use the present state of the advanced industrial "center" countries as the guiding model for the future. This is so for two reasons: in the first place, because of growing difficulties caused by the disproportional demands for investment capital, for industrial reconversion, and for competitive research and development, and the impossibility of servicing the foreign debt and stimulating internal growth at the same time; in the second place, because the social and cultural costs of an imitative development are too high and unethical under the pressure of the crisis. This crisis of directionality, however, is not resolved through deregulation. On the contrary, deregulation is simply the new version of development with a still-imitative model and, for the same reason, a specific directionality.

New political, economic, and technological conditions make ever-more difficult the desired confluence of individual projects in a joint project for the transformation of society. The progressive demystification of socialist experiences, the social disarticulation caused by the installation of repressive political regimes and by workforce recomposition, the substitution of insurrectional options by arranged or negotiated settlements in the resolution of political conflicts — these have taken the mobilizing force away from the idea of revolution. The proliferation of corporate interests, the disintegration of the traditional working-class image, the fragmentation of identities, which makes the unitary image of a "people" seem almost metaphysical, accelerating informalization, and the proliferation of the most varied strategies of survival — all of these factors weaken the formulation of global projects of structural change capable of motivating vast social sectors. Once again, however, the crisis does not suppose the collapse of but rather a challenge to planning. The collapse will occur when the crisis of projects leads to a kind of laziness disguised as pragmatism, in which politics is converted into the mere administration of crisis: an unethical and unaesthetic alternative.

Among the alternative proposals and/or perceptions that attempt to find a solution to the crisis of modernization in Latin America without identifying with the neoliberal program, it would be fitting to mention the following:

— The reappraisal of democracy for its intrinsic value and as an indispensable frame for dynamically joining a plurality of social interests and demands. Political theory certainly offers diverse conceptions of democracy. But faced with the growing complexity of the social fabric and the consequent crisis of authority, the kind of democracy posited as desirable is one based on extensive social agreement.[16] Such an agreement is conceived as a platform for resolving conflicts between sectors with a minimum of coercion and for articulating in the most harmonious way the relations between the state and civil society, the technical and political dimensions of development, planning and the market, the micro and the macro, and the local and the national. A democracy with articulatory capacity would permit the optimization of levels of social participation, the decentralization of decision-making processes, the apportionment of resources among the various agents of development, and the equitable distribution of the benefits of growth. Finally, a democracy founded on social agreement is the most appropriate means for encouraging a culture of civic coexistence that could conceive projects with social legitimacy.

— The reorientation of planning in tune with the new scenarios of social crisis and complexity. This supposes the relativization of mechanistic paradigms and requires working with growing levels of uncertainty about the future, open outcomes and ongoing, continuing adjustments, the activation and coordination of dispersed social energies, fields of multiple interaction, and mechanisms of cohesion that can articulate social projects without homogenizing.

— The change of perception and attitude of social scientists in the face of reality. In the decade of the sixties, the analytical exercise of sociology was, in good measure, determined by the idea of a "militant science" that was identified with a model of the state and social organization that projected an extreme normativism in questions of the styles of development. At present, a considerable number of social scientists in the region have opted for greater disciplinary humility, from which they seek to comprehend the complexity of dynamics that are created between multiple social actors. In a sense, the risk of global projects has been substituted by the "prudent" observation of intrasocietal articulations.[17]

— The reappraisal of social movements above political parties as protagonists in the rearticulation between civil society and the state.[18] Such an option follows from, in good measure, the relative incapacity of the traditional system of political parties to fulfill the function of mediation between social demands and the state apparatus. The crisis of the party system has given place to a search for new forms of doing politics, or at least for the diversification of political practices. In that context, social movements appear to be the bearers of new or different logics of collective interests, in contrast to the hierarchical uniformity that characterizes party organization. The reappraisal of social movements also aims to recover the richness of the social fabric as opposed to a state that has seldom taken it into account.

— The emergence of new social movments, or grassroots organizations, or "popular economic organizations," and the enthusiasm that this proliferation of initiatives awakens in some academicians and politicians disenchanted with conventional approaches to development.[19] These new social movements, as sociologists have taken to calling them, occupy sectors of informality that develop at the community, or local, level, and they are organized around collective strategies of survival or new forms of channeling demands. In practice, they combine diverse functions, such as the administration of scarcity, the mobilization of dispersed social energies, the de-hierarchization of production relations, the construction of collective identity, the socialized provision of basic necessities, the promotion of community participation, and the search for democracy in small spaces (or democracy in daily life). It is not easy to weigh the capacity of these movements to permeate the social fabric and to influence the technical and political leadership. Their emergence, however, posits a challenge, namely, to recuperate popular creativity and impel new "cultures" of development.

The postmodern debate can be fruitful in the sense that it permits, in general, the articulation of the cultural dimension of development. Its view of modernity allows us to interpret the crisis of styles of modernization as a cultural crisis. With this, new light is shed on the obscurity that presently envelops economic strategies and the policies of financial adjustment or control, and the discussion of policies and strategies is provided with a more comprehensive context from which it is possible to articulate immediate options in the operation of national projects or concrete utopias. The return to the cultural dimension of development permits the recreation of horizons that infuse politics and policies with a mobilizing force that convenes and commits social actors. The celebration of the new social movements shows a concern for the constitution of collective identities, be they regional or sectorial. The preference for social movements, as opposed to political parties, privileges new logics of social dynamism, the search for new forms of doing politics, and an ad hoc grounding of the exaltation of diversity. The reappraisal of democracy and pluralism points to the consolidation of a democratic culture and not only a majority-elected government. The reorientation of planning puts in place a change in paradigms of the interpretation and prediction of reality, and requires a revolution in perceptual structures, as well as in plans and programs. The reorientation of the social sciences also implies a change in the form of comprehending social reality, starting from the verification of the progressive complexity, increasing disarticulation, and polymorphism of the social fabric. In all of these forms of "groping in the dark," the tension between instrumental and substantive reason, or between means and ends, is once again at issue. Is this not, perhaps, one of the greatest cultural dilemmas of modernity? As we noted at the beginning, the postmodern debate may well be an attempt to remove the cultural base on which the road to modernization in Latin America has been constructed, be it successful or frustrated, open or truncated. But this does not necessarily imply that the invention of utopias and the design of projects has to be renounced, nor politics limited to laziness and the cynical administration of crisis. Nor does it mean that neoliberalism has to be embraced. On the contrary, it is through the thematic insistence on the cultural foundation of modernization that we can break with the neoliberal vicious circle and with shortsighted compulsion, often disguised as pragmatism.

Postmodernism requires that we open our perception to new contexts. Our battery of interpretive tools cannot remain unchanged faced with phenomena such as the acceleration of technological change, occupational recomposition, the deregulation of the financial system, the transnationalization of culture that accompanies the globalization of markets, social disarticulation, and the constriction of resources and margins of operation. Specifically, the challenge consists of enriching many of the concepts that, for a long time, permitted us to critically relate ourselves to modernity, with the aim of restoring their lost efficacy. The refunctioning of such concepts in the light of new times can lend great assistance for understanding our context and orienting our task. I am referring to concepts, or values, such as alienation, the satisfaction of social needs, structural change, social participation, personal development, social subjectivity, and emancipation from poverty and political oppression. None of these proves to be irrelevant or arbitrary today.

In the same way, it would not be sensible to renounce the interpretive and predictive richness of a structural focus on peripheral capitalism. This focus has permitted, in the past, the exercise of a notable critical and constructive capacity with respect to the styles of modernization implanted in Latin America and continues to encourage orientations and alternatives in the present.[20] Many of its suspicions and warnings regarding the models of development in force continue to be confirmed: the regressive tendency of the terms of exchange, the dynamic insufficiency of accumulation in peripheral capitalism, the difficulties of reconciling growth and equity, and structural heterogeneity.[21] Moreover, we do not possess another interpretive focus capable of giving a specific sense of totality and coherence to the heterogeneity characteristic of the processes of modernization in Latin America. Nevertheless, this focus cannot be taken as prescriptive. Its opening to the already mentioned problematic of social complexity or progressive uncertainty necessitates a critical revision of the mechanistic paradigm with which it usually operates.

In summary, the question we are considering here can be posed in the following terms: How can the postmodern debate be incorporated in order to reactivate the cultural basis of development, without it leading to the postmodernism functionally inherent in the neoliberalist project of political-cultural hegemony? How do we creatively confront our crisis of paradigms and projects, without this confrontation submerging us in a twilight "pathos" where the only option is the administration of entropy, the uncritical acceptance of a status quo that is critical of itself? How do we reinterpret the challenges of planning, the role of the state — and the program, or programs, of modernization — in light of this inevitable cultural earthquake announced by the postmodern trumpets? How can we integrate the critique of ethnocentrism (and along with it, the critique of imitative models of development) without leading to fantasies, fundamentalisms, regionalisms, particularisms, or other forms of wishful thinking?

The challenges and problems that are presented are very complex and can stimulate impotence as well as creativity. The multifaceted and structural character of the crisis situates us before a moment of maximum entropy that is, in turn, a moment of intensity. That is our weakness, but also our strength. In the throes of this dilemma, we go from enthusiasm to desperation, becoming postmoderns by osmosis in the midst of a still-pending modernization.

Notes

1 In the origin of the debate, Lyotard is the postmodern enthusiast — *The Postmodern Condition* (Minneapolis: University of Minnesota Press, 1985) — and Habermas the critical modernist — "Modernity, an Incomplete Project," in *The Anti-Aesthetic*, ed. Hal Foster (Port Townsend, Wash.: Bay Press, 1983), 3–15.

2 Baudrillard has been perhaps the most charismatic representative of this position.

3 "Postmodern culture does not guide or lead the process of secularization; it is its product. Specifically, it is the expression of a hypersecularization. Perhaps we should understand it as an ex post facto rationalization of a disenchantment." Norbert Lechner, "La democratización en el contexto de una cultura postmoderna," in *Cultura política y democratización*, ed. Norbert Lechner. Santiago: FLACSO/CLACSO/ICI, 1987, 253–62.

4 This, of course, was the lesson of Foucault. See Carlos Pareja, *Más allá del mito del progreso* (Montevideo: CLAEH, 1987); and Benjamin Arditi, "Una gramática postmoderna para pensar lo social," in Lechner, *Cultura política y democratización*, 169–88.

5 See, on this point, Octavio Paz, "The Twilight of the Avant-Garde," in *Children of the Mire* (Cambridge, Mass.: Harvard University Press, 1974), 148–64.

6 See Pedro Morandé, *Cultura y modernización en America Latina* (Santiago: Cuadernos del Instituto de Sociología/Pontificia Universidad Católica de Chile, 1984).

7 This negative evaluation of utopian thought was already present in the work of Karl Popper (e.g., *The Open Society and Its Enemies*, 5th ed. [London: Routledge and Kegan Paul, 1966]). In a different perspective, Franz Hinkelammert also undertakes a critique of specific forms of utopian thought in his *Crítica de la razón utópica* (San José, Costa Rica: DEI, 1984). See also my own "Construcción utópica y práctica política," *Revista Comunidad* 60 (1987): 3–11; and chapter 4 of this volume.

8 "But the dream of the abolition of state power no longer functions exclusively as part of the socialist vision of the future. On the other hand, on the right side of the political spectrum, there appeared a radical conceptualization of capitalism which supports similar concepts. This union of anarchism and capitalism . . . can be made plausible by the privatization of up to now state functions" (Hans Albert, quoted in Franz Hinkelammert, "Utopía y proyecto político: La cultura de la postmodernidad," *Revista Nueva Sociedad* 91 [1987]: 114–28).

9 In this sense, a postmodern vision of Latin America is provided by Hernando de Soto's best-seller, *El otro sendero* (Bogota: Editorial Oveja Negra, 1987), translated into English as *The Other Path* (New York: Harper and Row, 1989). In this book, the Peruvian economist analyzes the extensive informal economy of Peru and arrives at the conclusion that the variety of forms it displays, which are unfolding despite state regulation, gives evidence of the benefits of the market. In this way, de Soto transformed a problem, the informal sector, into a virtue, ignoring the vulnerability of resources and the poverty that accompanies the vast majority of the informal sector's population. The

book was heavily promoted in Latin America by neoliberal organizations and media, and Ronald Reagan mentioned it with enthusiasm in a speech.

10 We find an example of this in Joaquín Lavin's book, *La revolución silenciosa* (Santiago: Ed. Zig-Zag, 1987), another recent best-seller promoted by the neoliberal media. As in de Soto's book, Lavin elaborates a political-cultural strategy of market hegemony, appropriating terms that, in the past, were linked ideologically with the criticism of capitalism ("marginality," "informality," "revolution"), in order to redirect them as functional strategies for the expansion of the market.

11 "The everything goes [of postmodernism] is neither conservative, nor revolutionary, nor progressive. . . . In reality, what has triumphed is the cultural relativism which began its rebellion against the fossilization of class-cultures and against the ethnocentric dominance of an exclusive, correct, and authentic culture" (Agnes Heller, "Los movimientos culturales como vehículo de cambio," *Revista Nueva Sociedad* 96 [1988]: 44). In the article previously cited, Lechner observes, "postmodern culture assumes hypersecularization in its tendency to separate social structures from value and motivational structures. That is, it accepts the liberal vision of politics as a market: an exchange of goods. And what happens to nonexchangeable goods? I am referring to human rights, psycho-social necessities such as social roots and collective belonging, the necessity of transcendental referents, but also to fear and the desire for certainty. I do not see any consideration of this in postmodern culture" (258). But Lechner also shares Heller's vision of the value of the relativizing function that postmodern discourse can exercise in the face of ideological and political reductionism.

12 Among them are included some figures already mentioned here (Arditi, Lechner, Pareja, Baudrillard, and Lyotard) and others from the Anglo-Saxon world, such as Hal Foster, Craig Owens, and Fredric Jameson.

13 On this point, see the classic essays: Max Horkheimer and Theodor W. Adorno, "The Dialectic of Enlightenment" and Max Horkheimer, "A Critique of Instrumental Reason," in their *Dialectic of Enlightenment* (New York: Herder and Herder, 1972).

14 On this point, see the papers from the ILPES (Instituto Latinoamericano y del Caribe de Planificación Económica y Social), *Revista de la CEPAL* 31 (1987); and Carlos Matus, *Planificación de situaciones* (Caracas: CENDES).

15 No one can doubt that the same transnational corporations, in large measure linked to the crisis of state planning (and the most enthusiastic about this crisis), plan all the time and invest considerable sums for this purpose. The strategy for the acceleration of technological change and for growing diversification of products responds to an attentive job of planning by the transnationals.

16 There is much literature that points in this direction. The following examples are noteworthy: Norbert Lechner, *La conflictiva y nunca acabada construcción del orden deseado* (Santiago: Ediciones Ainavillo, FLACSO, 1984); Angel Flisifisch, "Consenso democrático en el Chile autoritario," in Lechner, *Cultura política y democratización,* 99–128; Norbert Lechner (comp.), *Estado y política en América Latina* (Mexico: Siglo

XXI, 1981), and Gino Germani et al., *Los límites de la democracia* (Buenos Aires: CLACSO, 1985).

17 The influence of Alain Touraine is well known in this tendency in Latin America. Touraine posits that the reorientation of sociology towards the comprehension of social actors coincides with the political reappraisal of democracy. See his *Le Retour de l'acteur* (Paris: Fayard, 1984).

18 See, for example, Elizabeth Jelin (comp.), *Movimientos sociales y democracia emergente* (Buenos Aires: Centro Editor de América Latina, 1987); Alain Touraine, *Nuevas pautas de acción colectiva en América Latina* (Santiago: PREALC, 1984); Fernando Calderón (comp.), *Los movimientos sociales ante la crisis* (Buenos Aires: CLACSO 1986); Fernando Calderón and Mario R. dos Santos, "Movimientos sociales y gestación de cultura política: Pautas de interogación," in Lechner, *Cultura política y democratización*, 189–98; and Enzo Faletto, "Propuestas para el cambio: Movimientos sociales en la democracia," in *Revista Nueva Sociedad* 91 (1987): 141–47.

19 For example, see Tilman Evers, "Identidade: A face oculta dos novos movimentos sociais," in *Novos Estudos CEBRAP* (1984), 11–15; José Luis Castagnola, *Participación y movimientos sociales* (Montevideo: *Cuadernos de CLAEH* 39, 1986); Luis Razeto, *Economía de solidaridad y mercado democrático*, two vols. (Santiago: Programa de Economía del Trabajo, 1984–1985); Luis Razeto et al., *Las organizaciones económicas populares* (Santiago: Programa de Economía del Trabajo, 1983); *Development Dialogue*, special issue (Dec. 1986); and Martín Hopenhayn, "Nuevos enfoques sobre el sector informal," *Pensamiento Iberoamericano* 12 (July–Dec. 1987): 423–28.

20 For example, see the recent works of Osvaldo Sunkel, such as "Las relaciones centroperiferia y la transnacionalización," *Pensamiento Iberoamericano* 11 (Jan.–June 1987).

21 In the extensive bibliography of Raul Prebisch, the following texts deserve to be cited here: "Estructura económica y crisis del sistema," *Revista de la CEPAL* (1978): 167–264, and the book *Capitalismo periférico: Crisis y transformación* (Mexico: Fondo de Cultura Económica).

7 ✳ The Crisis of Legitimacy of the Planning State

State Crisis as Sociocultural Crisis

For some time now the image of the Planning State in Latin America has been weakening from various flanks. This State as Demiurge (the God of Creation, according to Platonic and Alexandrian philosophy; the all-soul, active world principle, according to the Gnostics), leader in modernization, impartial referee in social conflicts and great political totalizer, is the target of objections from all sides: it's utopian or instrumentalist, too eratic or too rigid, capitalist or an obstacle to capitalism, vulnerable or hypertrophied. It is argued that its very conception was an error, illusion, or failure, or that the crisis of the 1980s—the ensuing decade lost to development and its consequences, played out in all fields—demolished a project that was, until the 1970s, still the functional formula for the partial modernization of mixed economies. The Planning State is attacked from the new right and from the new left, from ideology, from economics, and from ideology funneled into economics, as well as from politics and culture.

According to how the State is defined we can situate the crisis of the Planning State into a range of possible perspectives. If the State is conceived as the *expression of the antagonism of interests* between distinct social sectors, for example, then the crisis of the Planning State need be traced to its inability to regulate the access of distinct social sectors to socially produced resources. If the State is conceived as a *bureaucratic machine,* the crisis of the Planning State can be associated with the hypertrophy of the public apparatus, or with the tensions between the bureaucratic logic of the State and the multiple logics of civil society (in its productive, communicational, consensual aspects, and so forth). If the state is designed as a *meta-actor,* that is to say, as a political authority capable of bringing into harmony and leading the whole of society along the path of modernization and development, the crisis of the Planning State obeys the disturbances that global changes (industrial, financial, and commercial) generate in national economies. At the same time, that crisis corresponds to excessive social and structural heterogeneity in societies that are meant to be "molded" by the State's integrating action.

This multifaceted fracture of the Planning State, as an image and as utopia, has run off the cliff, along with the tradition of State planning that was so promising in the region in the dawning of the 1960s. Together with the *large-scale politics* of the State, *large-scale social engineering* has similarly crashed. The ravine which crisis cleft has swallowed both the dream of the State-planned utopia, as well as the dream of the utopic or universalized planner. In the various forms of comprehending the crisis, the Planning State is split wide, and the legitimacy of State planning gravely diminished. That crisis is conceived as a loss of collective direction, an inability to integrate/modernize society through state action, an inability to assign resources rationally among different social sectors, or as a conflict between the technical rationalization imposed by planning and the social claims and defenses pushing civil society towards the State. The loss of legitimacy is particularly difficult to resolve when it's produced by the internal contradiction between the two sources of legitimacy, for planning and the Planning State in general. On one side, there's the legitimacy acquired through *expertise* in making decisions. On the other side is the legitimacy originating in social support or consensus. This necessity of double legitimization, as technically competent and as socially representative of the aspirations of the actors, is necessarily twisted, over and over. This occurs mainly when the State's disposable resources shrink, or when struggles over interests in society become more acute.

Such contradiction historically falls into diverse forms or molds. One such form or mold is the overextension of technical legitimacy, with political legitimacy consequently minimized. To this is opposed another, equally or even more frequently occurring form: the politicization of the technical corps, whose knowledge is appropriated by political engineering in order to fabricate the adherence of the citizenry to a political force or government. In this case the planner turns into a kind of organic intellectual whose *expertise* is subordinated to the will to power, or the will to political legitimization. State life in Latin America hasn't been—nor is it now—a life of reasonable equilibrium between these two sources of legitimacy. The bias of the technocrats or of political clienteles are more strained than harmonized.

Planning is not just halfway between technical legitimization and legitimization by consensus, between expertise and political belief. It also sees strains between public management and private economic agents (as well as between distinct agents within the public apparatus itself). On one side, political leadership reproaches the planners for being biased towards technology and repeatedly calls for greater political functionality. On the other side, the private business sector reproaches public planners in the event of any kind of "politicizing butt-insky." This conflictive situation illustrates, in cartoon-like fashion, how in the model of the Planning State, planning has served as a hinge, situated between the government and social actors, technical discourse and political discourse, science and the will to power, the public project and the private interest.

Associating planning with a determinate *image* of the State allows for the recontextualization of a crisis normally dealt with solely from an economic angle. The act of putting into relief the hinge-like nature which planning assumes, at least in the libretto, makes it possible to conceive the crisis of the Planning State in sociocultural terms: as a tension between rationalities (instrumental versus political, formal versus substantive); as the nonarticulation of actors (be they the State versus society, intrasocietal, or intra-State fragmentation); as the tension of logics (bureaucratic versus technocratic, for example); or as friction between spaces (the public versus the private, the national versus the international, the local versus the national).

To explain the crisis of the Planning State in terms of legitimacy also allows for a sociocultural interpretation of the crisis, in which the phenomena can be comprehended from various optics: from the power of seduction and conviction that the *image* of the Planning State is capable of exercising; from the effectiveness at mobilizing and bringing together the masses, on the part of this State or its image; as the collective adherence to an ideology of development, to an institutionalized form of political guidance, and to a certain historical directionality; and as the organic connection which the State is capable of establishing between the production of social wisdom and the use of this wisdom for the transforming intervention of social reality. A sociocultural dimension of development is very present in all of these senses.

My intention in this chapter is to probe the wounded face of the Planning State, a face that is wounded in its image and in its history. I'm interested in singling out its problems of legitimacy, which did not begin with, but were exacerbated by the crises of the 1980s. In so doing, I hope to add something to the interpretations of those who persist in the struggle to understand the political-cultural atmosphere in which we are immersed, which leads me, in turn, to dig into some of the historical contradictions by way of which blood continuously drains from the image of the Planning State.

The Utopia of the Planning State in Latin America

There's been much reflection on the central role that the State has played in the modernization and development processes of the majority of countries in Latin America. The currency or pertinence of such centrality is much questioned today. If the State is the leading agent in the development and the directionality that it assumes, the modality as much as the magnitude of its intervention are increasingly subject to debate. The present restriction of financial flows, the greater efficiency that private enterprise shows in some fields, and the international economy's increasingly decentralized forms of insertion are all factors that cannot leave unscathed the role of the State in the region. Yet each time that we explain the capacities of the Planning State — as historical project and experiment — it seems necessary to go back to the long-standing problems of articulation between the Planning State and civil society, problems that the Planning State, with its multiple functions and elevated self-image, hinted at solving.

The peripheral, dependent, late-development condition of countries in Latin America led the State to acquire, from very early on, decisive functions in the enterprise of modernization and development.[1] The recognized necessity of transforming an agrarian and mining-based society organized as an oligarchy into an urban-industrial society with a dynamic entrepreneurial class, and which would be less vulnerable to the economic dynamism of the centers, brought the State to take on a leading role in the processes of capitalist modernization. This led it to take a wide range of functions into its own hands. Among them, the following can't be omitted:

— to generate a productive modern apparatus that would permit the substitution of imports and competitively integrate itself into international commerce;

— to integrate the national population on the basis of a structure with a strongly urban bias, which promotes formal employment and executes an infrastructure requiring titanic investments;

— to redistribute part of the benefits of growth for the sake of the general welfare and greater social integration, above all through expanding free education, by opening access to health services, and through the generalized provision of basic services, as in the creation of a general system of social security and of labor legislation;

— to reconcile the diverse interests of social actors or economic agents that are reconstituted in the heat of modernization;

— to bring capitalist development into harmony within the distinct sectors and branches of activity throughout the country's different regions.

In consequence, and as Enzo Faletto warns, "the simple verification of the importance that the State takes on, in Latin America, leads to the postulate that the State prevails over civil society, which is to say that the State is not just the political expression of the society and the power existing in that society, but that it furthermore organizes the whole of the society. . . . a brief review of the contemporary history of Latin America is sufficient to realize how the action of the State has been almost decisive for the makeup of the urban-industrial system, which has resulted in a greater development and complexity of civil society."[2] Adolfo Gurrieri similarly indicates that when the problem of state intervention is posed in Latin America (amid the crises of the 1930s and later, during World War II), the tasks have encompassed an integration at once physical, economic, and social. Within the region, the role of the State thus projected was more ambitious than what was then attributed to the newborn Welfare State in the developed world. It tried to integrate the marginalized, to bring harmony to the integrated, and, at the same time, to face the rest of the world with progressive autonomy: "The State being a decisive agent in that process, the model reflected by the Welfare State and Keynesian forms of intervention were manifestly insufficient. The role of the State in Latin America would have to be wider and deeper than in the central countries. Although the latter were in the middle of a grave crisis, they didn't have to face the transformation of the pattern of growth, the economic and political integration of profoundly heterogeneous structures, or the productive absorption of wide contingents coming from precapitalist modes of production."[3]

The planned Latin American State was paradigmatically conceived by CEPAL to face the challenges of development in the region.[4] This conception was partly the *invention* of an unprecedented concept of the State, and partly the *discovery* of a type of State that had been insinuating itself throughout Latin America since the 1930s. In other words, *the model of the Planning State was the consistent and unitary theoretical reconstruction of what was already going on, in a discontinuous manner, and in day-to-day practice.* The multifunctional primacy of this paradigmatic State in Latin America not only extended to the leading role of the State in economic undertakings and activities. It turned the State, simultaneously, into a demiurge and synthesis of civil society, into a Great Conductor and a Great Articulator, into a *meta-actor* (who coordinates and arbitrates the different social agents in the process of development) and into a *mega-actor* (who concentrates a good part of the national economic activity). The following definition gives an idea of this totalizing vision that the State assumes when it is adjusted to the normative model of the Planning State: "An institution relatively independent of society and of classes, not subject to the coercion of competition in the market or the necessity for appreciation of capital. The State can and should present itself as the universal instance and incarnation of the collective interest. . . . This dynamic is unfolded and revealed across a range of functions that the State assumes. . . . It is the producer of legitimacy and consensus for its own power and for the system. . . . It reinforces and readjusts its politico-administrative apparatus of domination and its functions of social coercion, its means of violence and of control . . . it unifies and integrates the country. It is the co-producer, co-presenter and co-disseminator of culture and ideology, of technology and of science, and the direct manager or influential regulator for the formation of human resources. In its relations between the country and the international system, it mediates and arbitrates between national and foreign groups, between national autonomy and external dependency."[5]

In the original thought of ECLAC (Economic Commission for Latin America and the Caribbean) this State, understood as mega-actor and meta-actor, appears as endowed with a surprising diversity of strengths:

internal unity and coherency, autonomy facing other agents, political and economic power, technical-administrative and management capacity, and the control of external economic relations. The rank of meta-actor that the State occupies in this maximalist model locates it over and above the social actors or economic agents, arbitrating interclass and intersector conflicts, assuming the most important challenges of economic investment and accumulation, and reconciling interests that are displaced and that confront the compass of modernization guided by the State itself. In addition to this, and owing to the emphasis on the planning character of said State, the State impregnates society with an economic rationality (or modern rationality, often assumed as synonymous with economic rationality), simultaneously turning it into the incarnation of an Enlightenment and instrumental project. It rationalizes the conduct of all the social actors so that they function in terms of the State's own previously defined, supposed directionality of progress.

How is planning yoked to a State with an instrumentalist and Enlightenment bias, to which is attributed the faculty of marking directionality for the whole of society, based on economic rationalization? In other words, if planning constitutes a defining characteristic of this paradigmatic State (in as much as it is defined as the Planning State), and this State is constituted, in its turn, as mega-actor and as meta-actor: what role does planning fill?

The role of the planner becomes strategic in this context: as one who articulates the political and the economic (or consensus and effectiveness; the private and the public; and the different instances within the public sector that attract and invest the State's resources). The role of the planner is to reinforce the State's character as both mega-actor and meta-actor. To do so involves resorting to instrumental control, whose ultimate objective could be defined, in the best enlightened-technical fashion, as *socioeconomic rationalization of a process of integration and development aimed at the attainment of objectives previously agreed on by the political power of the State and legitimated, in greater or lesser measure, by the consent of the citizens.*

The same enlightened emphasis on directionality (in the sense of attainment of ultimate objectives) appears in the following definition of planning, understood as "technical support to socially legitimated political leadership, so that the outcome of decentralized decisions allows for the reduction of uncertainty regarding a country's future."[6] Three elements turn out to be crucial in this conception of planning: the tension or combination of technical with political reason; functionality for a socially legit-imated power; and the tension between control and uncertainty regarding the future. This definition is meaningful for the most mundane functions of planning, such as regulating and limiting the patterns of accumulation among private agents by means of customs duties, monetary and taxation policies; for redistributing the profits from development by means of social policies; and for privileging strategic productive sectors by means of policies aimed at orienting and planning public undertakings.[7]

Evaluation, negotiation, regulation, coordination and redistribution are tasks appropriate to planners in their roles as individuals meant to articulate between the public and the private, and the technical and the political. Insofar as what has been defined here as the paradigmatic State constitutes a multifunctional apparatus that orients modernization and development, its legitimacy depends, in great measure, on its demon-strated capacity to closing the gap between the *directionality* that it pre-scribes to the whole of society and the means that it mobilizes to accom-plish this effectively. That gap is resolved, at least theoretically, by the technical-practical arsenal of planning.

If the State assumes the status of meta-actor (harmonizer of the claims and interests of the many actors composing the social fabric), and if it also acquires the rank of mega-actor (through the size of its apparatus and its weighty, influential role within the economy), it can only socially legiti-mate this position by offering, to civil society, an exemplary model of dynamism, efficiency, coordination and competency in its undertakings. Planning would be called to fulfill, at least ideally, the decisive function of providing state power with pertinent procedures for preserving that type of legitimacy.[8]

Penetrating the contradictions of the Planning State allows an explana-tion of the crisis of that State from two angles: according to how it is articulated within civil society (as State-Conductor) and according to its own rationality (as State-Apparatus). State intervention has had both of these meanings in Latin America, and it has been inherent to development in the region ever since the changing of the guard, when, in the 1930s, distinct versions of the populist State took over from the oligarchic State. State intervention has been particularly strong since it took on the wide-spread strategy of industrialization and import-substitution. The crisis of the interventionist model, as the most enthusiastic anti-Statists diagnose it, obeys various circumstances, among which the following stand out: the stagnation provoked by the exaggerated statization of economic life; the tendency to reduce spaces for private enterprise on behalf of public enterprise; the distortions that "State capitalism" generates in the internal market, above all for the application of policies of protectionism; and the overload of social claims assumed by the populist State in virtue of a symbolic social pact for development.[9] Objections to the concrete forms of State intervention also appear from a less neoliberal position, indicating that the State in Latin America tends to cronyism, to the hypertrophy of the public sector, to the corporatization of State enterprises, and that such a State is more a legalistic than a legitimated entity, suffering an endemic crisis of representation.

For all the possible validity of the objections noted above, these do no more than trigger an underlying contradiction that sooner or later need be fully manifest. I refer to the contradiction between an ideal paradigm, of the Planning State versus the historically materialized institution. Even though this difference might seem an obvious point for reflection, it hasn't been entirely explicit in the din of public discourse. It is hard to estimate how this confusion could contribute to the progressive discrediting of the State. The gap produced between the model posed as *utopian referent* and the real and concrete State tends to reproduce itself, between the image that the State has projected towards (or "offered to") society, and the State which that society has seen in action. Here, the idea I venture is that within its own public discourse the State projected, as idea and as image of itself, not so much its effective possibilities as the enlightenment utopia of a State towering over society by the sidereal flight of reason and progress. This reduction of the State to its ideal image also fell back onto planning, in that in planning it sought the ability to close the gap between the Utopian and real State. The present crisis doubtless made more acute the problems that planning dragged along with it, beginning with its conception within the bosom of the Planning State in Latin America.[10]

The fissures open along two flanks: widening the gap between the idealized image of the Planning State and its conflictive, historical routine, resulting in a "retroactive" action in this gap, eroding the *very image* and *very rationality* originally projected by the Planning State. The widening of the gap as much as the deterioration and questioning of the very image and rationality of the Planning State constitute problems with strong sociocultural tradition. The pages that follow put the contrasts into relief, between the paradigmatic-utopian image projected by the State and its effective historical reality.

Crisis of the Planning State: The irreconcilable gap between image and reality

Reality took over, making manifest the insuperable contradictions in the collision between the facts and the aspirations to multifunctionality. Neither the agents nor the eventual beneficiaries of the model perceived, however, the failure of the Planning State as a utopian impossibility or as a gap between a maximalist image and a conflictive reality. Utopia was internalized — and *disguised* — from the start, as a program or as a task to be completed. So were the inefficiencies of the Planning State filed away as "a failure in the program," rather than as an index of the impossibility of molding an ideal order. It's certain that part of the failure, if it can be called that, corresponds to errors or shortcomings that could be avoided in practice. *But the name of "failure" disguises the natural distance between a paradigmatic reference and a concrete project.*

The gap between theoretical construction and real experience opened up from three sides: as a gap between the image of an ideal State of great internal coherence and a real State in which rationalities coexist in tension; as a gap between the harmonic image of a State dynamically articulated with civil society (call it social actors, economic agents, and/or classes), and a real articulation marked by permanent conflicts; and as a gap between the utopian image of a solid State, endowed with a great capacity for maneuvering, and a real, vulnerable State, very much exposed to the effects of changing scenarios, international as much as internal. I will try, in the following, to sketch out a descriptive map of these gaps.

The gap between internal coherency and internal fragmentation. The gap between a State with great internal coherence, as conceived from the utopia of the Planning State, and its crystallization in a State rubbed by the juxtaposed logics in its own apparatus, can be summarized in three types of tension appearing within the State: tensions between technical and political rationality; tensions between technocracy and bureaucracy, and tensions between coercive and orienting directionality.

The tension between technification and politicization opposes the conventional figure of the planner to that of the politician.[11] The stereotype of the planner operates with instrumental criteria, based on the calculation of disposable means and the optimal coordination of economic and social policies. The logic of the politician is, instead, principally oriented towards the conflict and competition of social forces, and towards creating optimal civic adherence. The State's political leadership has frequently capitalized on planning in order to compete in proposing electoral pro-grams. It isn't easy to estimate the degree to which this aspect of planning's functionality for political competition is foreign to the technical rationality of planning. Nor is it easy to indicate the measure to which the relation between planning and government action is marked by complementarity or by conflict. It's not that planning would be politically aseptic, as a rule. As has historically been the case, today it isn't easy to collate its technical inclination with the political functionality that governments and parties often request of it in practice.

The tension between technocrats and bureaucrats has already been indi-cated as a problem of the Planning State and an obstacle for the success of the experiences of planning in the region. José Medina Echavarría's already classic text offers a substantial analysis of the conflict between bureaucratic and technocratic utopias in planning, indicating that in both cases the utopian resides in the *claim* that the power implicated in the planning process will be concentrated within a single social support, whether bu-reaucracy or technocracy. Bureaucratic utopia is rooted in expanding and consolidating rational administration aimed at enabling and sustaining the formation of the modern State and economic development. Technocratic utopia, on its part, grants self-sufficient value to science and to technique, working from the supposition that society can be molded and oriented in accordance with the plan drafted by the experts. Both utopias put two requirements for hegemonic conquest into practice: the acceptance or imposition of its intellectual supremacy, and political supremacy with re-gard to other groups similarly engaged in struggling for hegemony.[12]

The Planning State has experienced much difficulty in making these two logics fit together. While the power of bureaucracy is justified from within by its suitability to institutional norms and its capacity to perpetuate them, the power of technocracy rests on its supposed competency for sketching technical outlines from within the State apparatus. In the case of a model of the State to which the function of conducting the process of modernization is attributed, the transformations generated in that very modernization provoke collisions between the institutional and technical frameworks. Such collisions tend to be expressed in intra-State non-coordination, bogged down decision processes, and the non-articulation between eco-nomic and political organizations.

The State's lack of internal cohesion becomes more palpable when the State's distinct functions or definitions are associated with divergent inter-ests. In this way, we can see the State as an actor in itself, with its own interests and benefits and its own form of economic insertion in national life. It can also appear as the political superstructure of private sectors that possess greater power within the interior of civil society, sectors towards whom the State establishes favorable mechanisms. Finally, it can appear as a national State or social totalizer (or as a conductor of development and national unity). In this way, privileging objectives which are of general interest or of interest for multiple sectors of society, *State Apparatus, Capitalist State* and *National State* are, simultaneously, three in one. In the decision processes there is no previous "distribution" of the three identities at stake, but rather a constant rivalry on the part of the concrete subjects that compose the State, seeking to impose the interest of the bureaucrat, the dominant groups, or the nation.

The fissures within the Planning State consequently open up, between distinct rationalities (technical versus political, bureaucratic versus technocratic), between different actors (political, planners, public functionaries), and between the diverse interests of the bureaucrat, the capitalist, and the nation. The State's loss of internal consistency directly corresponds to a loss of consistent directionality that the State prescribes and in which it takes a leading role with respect to the loss of the ability to direct the development process. With respect to, or together with society, the State becomes less efficient as it becomes less articulated; its loss of legitimacy accelerates as the image it projects towards civil society increasingly crumbles. In failing to reconcile the interests within its own apparatus, the State's internal disarticulation leads to its increased vulnerability to exogenous pressures, be they national or international.[13]

The gap between harmonic integration and endemic conflict. The image of harmony that the utopia of the Planning State projects with respect to the articulation of the State and civil society contrasts with a historical reality full of ongoing conflicts between the two spheres. Those conflicts are continually intertwined. The following pages try to summarize each separately, so that they may be more discernible.

A first form that the conflict assumes is between policies that privilege economic growth alone, versus policies that prioritize the social redistribution of that growth. While the Planning State proposed combining economic growth and the redistribution of its proceeds as its central objective, modernization made society's internal conflicts more acute. Struggles over distribution turned into acute political confrontations. The economic growth of the region has led to patterns of development which generate tremendous imbalances and social inequalities, and consequently marked degrees of conflict. The State is resultingly put in a difficult position: on the one hand it has had to attend to popular demands and expectations, but on the other hand it cannot confront groups with greater economic power.

Capitalist modernization allowed (and required) the consolidation of a national bourgeoisie that, in their turn, demanded that the State preserve the rules of play functioning towards its expansion. Just as those same bourgeoisie saw the State strengthened, as a dynamic agent of development, they objected to the redistributive mechanisms that the State tried to promote in order to give development a national scope. This was translated into economic and political pressures from the most robust economic sectors, destined to block the democratization of the fruits of growth. On the other extreme of the social spectrum, the Planning State conducted a modernizing process that generated a spiral of requirements and demands in the popular sectors, often accompanied by high degrees of social and political mobilization. The crisis of governability resulting from these counterpoised pressures progressively weakened the legitimacy of the State and eroded its capacity to conduct development processes.

Another form of explaining the conflict is by way of the contradiction between the transformational versus the preservative functions of the Planning State. Structural changes could come from the will of the State, by virtue of its integrative vocation and by way of capitalist modernization's inability to incorporate productive employment and the benefits of growth throughout all social sectors. Or, structural changes could be the result of growing social pressures within the frame of dual (or heterogeneous) societies with tremendous socio economic contrasts. In either case, the conflict between the option of *growing without transforming* versus *transforming in order to integrate* puts the State at the center of an acute confrontation. The image of the State as meta-actor — that is to say, the authority capable of bringing harmony to the claims of diverse social actors — contrasts, then, with the image of a State which social actors take as a strategic instrument to be appropriated in order to impose a particular project onto society (a project that represents "non-universalizable" interests).

A third contradiction emerges from the former, occurring in real events: namely, the incompatibility of a State that offers itself as conductor of development with a State turned into the battle scenario for social interests in confrontation.[14] In Latin America the heterogeneous configuration of societies, halfway between the modern and the traditional, and the social fragmentation that this implies weakens the intermediary organizations, so that they fail to fulfill the decisive, mediatory role that they fulfill in modern societies. Because of this, we find ourselves with societies appealing to the State for the resolution of their conflicts from all corners, be they regional, local, or sector- or labor-related.

This generates a paradoxical situation where very heterogeneous and fragmented societies show themselves to be, in turn, highly politicized. Facing this picture, in which the claims of the most diverse sectors and the echoes of the most varied conflicts come together, the State becomes the boxing ring that society uses for arbitrating its differences. It is difficult to revive the image of the State-conductor, from under the ropes of the State as boxing ring.

The problem becomes even more complex when the informal sector is introduced into the analysis, because the informal sector has no organic channels for pressuring the State, except for what that sector most often manages to accomplish by its mere presence, which overflows all institutionalization that the State has projected. On one hand, the State seems *inundated* by the divergent interests of actors with the power to make themselves present within the apparatus and within public space. On the other hand, the same State appears to be *excluding* informal actors who are spread out across the base of the social fabric.

A fourth tension comes from the Planning State's claim to modernize and bring harmony at the same time, to the whole of social sectors and economic agents. In its quality as conductor of the process of modernization, the State has appropriated not only the function of transforming the productive structure, but also of guaranteeing that this process would integrate the country from within as well as from without, so that it revolves around the axis of industrialization. This enterprise has proven fruitless in fact. Working from a metasocial instance such as the Planning State attempts, the idea of rationally regulating society aimed at granting a harmonious cohesion shatters against a global tendency towards sociocultural fragmentation.[15]

That tendency towards fragmentation takes on dramatic and exacerbated indications in present-day Latin America. On the one side, the type of economic growth propelled since the end of World War II has not produced the trickle down effect necessary to eliminate the distortions characteristic of so-called peripheral-dependent capitalist economies. The extensive literature regarding the segmented distribution of earnings, urban marginality in the 1960s, and the informal sector in the 1970s and 1980s amply shows the structural obstacles to "harmonious" modernizing integration. On the other side, the policies of adjustment advanced from the 1980s have generated extremely high social costs, where the distribution of sacrifices tends to be ever more regressive. Finally, the anti-Statist excesses of the market offensive have strangled redistributive functions of the State that traditionally operated as efficient vehicles of social integration.

The difficulties that the Planning State faces with regard to modernizing, integrating, and bringing harmony all at the same time are also aggravated by the transnationalization of the economy and of the culture. The recomposition of the center-periphery articulation as an effect of the logic of the transnationals presents two new elements, namely: "a) a complex of activities, social groups, and regions, that find themselves geographically located in different Nation-States, yet which make up the developed part of the global system and that are closely interconnected, transnationally, through a variety of concrete interests, by similar lifestyles and levels of life and strong political and sociocultural affinities; and b) a national complement of activities, social groups, and subordinated regions, partially or totally marginalized from that part of the nation which has developed from the global system, and which has no tie to similar activities, groups, or regions in other nations."[16]

In this way, the transnational pattern consecrates a world where the borders of Nation-States are cut off by the division between *the transnationalized and the integrated,* on one hand, and *the marginalized and the dispersed,* on the other hand. The integrated make up a *hegemonic* economy and a *hegemonic* culture. For the marginalized, subculturization and economic insertion are subordinated from within, and are inwardly heterogeneous: this is where the members of the informal sector, the members of regional ethnic groups, the less-specialized wage earners and the urban and rural marginalized live.

While the integrated share the communicative codes, consumption habits, and sensibilities of their peers in the industrialized world, in the world of the excluded a culture of insecurity is lived, which is resolved by codes of violence, solidarity, or seclusion (or a combination of these). The gap between the codes of the integrated and of the excluded cannot be closed up by way of the common denominator of television consumption, for the growing frustration in the expectations of the non-integrated sectors regarding the benefits of modernization grows all the more when they observe on a daily basis the contrast between their lives and the lives of those who are surely galloping along in the chariot of material progress. The costs of this stratification aren't just ethical and cultural: they can also have negative repercussions on social peace and political governability.

The high rates of economic informality and social marginality registered in the populations of most of the countries of the region show the broadly utopian aspect of the Planning State's willingness to integrate. With its wide array of survival employment, familiar life strategies, quasi-legal activities and marginal, interstitial or communitarian forms of economic organization, informality has little to do with the kind of modernizing integration paradigmatically designed in the project of the Planning State.[17] This occurs, in part, because of the conditions of poverty in which the majority of the informal sector in the region unfolds, aggravating the socioeconomic contrasts of Latin American societies and gravely impeding integration by way of equitable redistribution of the proceeds of growth. It also occurs because those from the informal sector (or the marginalized, according to the type of activity or settlement emphasized) *culturally* and *politically* constitute *the other*, and are always indigestible for the dialectic of progress. What remains, not subordinated to the system of political parties, not taken up into an articulated commitment to the State, not given to public spaces, not reliant on the classical services of the Welfare State, muddies up social and work statistics.

The integrating vocation assumed up by the Planning State shatters as it comes up against the irrefutable reality of the informal world and of the poor. The harmony contained in the dream of social integration falls apart in the harshness of a grainy insomnia. The myth of coherence is inundated by the law of fragmentation, thus revealing its very nature, that is, its mythic character. With crisis, that badly named "invisible world" becomes intolerably visible to those who maintain the pretension of inhabiting integrated societies. *The exteriorization of the submerged,* a phenomenon that the economic crisis of the 1980s has precipitated throughout most Latin American countries, has undermined, in a deaf and wholly systematic fashion, the expectations for societal synthesis deposited, once upon a time, in the Great State.

The Planning State's unfolding between the capitalist and the national State obliged it to take on functions not readily reconciled: namely, to serve, on one hand, as a instrument for the consolidation of a national entrepreneurial class and to conduct, on the other hand, a national process of social integration. It frequently happens that the entrepreneurs' interests are not "universalizable" or capable of encompassing all social actors in a determined moment. On one part, the Capitalist State recognizes entrepreneurs as economic agents who operate as central conductors of development, but at the same time, as a National State it must require specific behaviors rarely accepted without resistance from that entrepreneurial sector, such as an attitude of investment rather than of consumption, of austerity rather than squandering, of utilizing resources with a sense of social responsibility rather than of individual gain. Inversely, as a National State it must support the demands of less integrated sectors, who have less access to goods and to services, promoting a recovery occurring especially by way of redistribution policies, social policies, or employment policies that can enter into open contradiction with short-term interests of the more privileged sectors. But inasmuch the State is a capitalist one, it must subordinate its integrating interventionism to the dynamism of the modern capitalist sector, especially to those who have the greatest decision making power within this sector.

The tension between classist and universalist State (or capitalist and national State) sooner or later appears in the processes of modernization. This especially appears with the spiraling expectations that it generates as it aspires to integrate wider and wider sectors into the benefits of progress (or, into *hoping* for the benefits of progress). The following reference is very clear in this respect: "The State places itself in front of classes as the guarantor and organizer of social relations that constitute classes as such, on which account . . . it is also the guardian of the subordinated classes. . . . First, making the pretension of being a State 'for everyone' seem more real . . . second, promoting living conditions for the subordinated classes which are more or less compatible, in each historical instance, with the current relations between the production and accumulation of capital. . . . But—and this is the other term of the ambiguity— . . . the eventual impossibility of satisfying the demands put forward . . . can put 'excessive' stress on the accumulation of capital."[18]

In contrast to the image of continuity that it has wanted to project, the Planning State thus appears shaken by permanent discontinuity. As a National State, it only gradually integrates those whom development has brushed aside and left behind if it functions according to the dynamic of the more socially powerful capitalist sectors. If that integration runs counter to that "non universalizable" dynamic of the capitalist agents, however, then it might turn back or be interrupted. The previously mentioned case of growing global, intranational and international division of the integrated versus the marginalized shows the point to which the conduct of the most dynamic sectors, often backed up by the National States themselves, can run counter to social integration within a country.

The paradox in which this double function of the Planning State is finished off is rooted in the fact that the State *plans capitalism,* that is to say, "it constructs" a capitalist society almost from the State itself. Central planning in mixed economies, which has been the predominant tone in Latin America, precisely responds to said will.[19] From this perspective, and as Gurrieri warns in the article already cited, the crisis of the Planning State occurs when a project in play has been one of "planned capitalism" that, among other things, counted on minimal discipline from private enterprise, the entrepreneurs being dynamic agents privileged by planning itself. With that the conflict mentioned in the previous point reappears — that is, when it functions as a capitalist State, it is exposed to the sudden and unexpected attacks of the entrepreneurial class.

A sixth tension comes given by the character of mega-actor of the State, that is, for the considerable dimension which the State takes on as an economic agent by way of its own entrepreneurial activity. In this case the State/market conflicts don't come from the State's regulating emphasis on the market, but from the dispute between public and private enterprise. In this way, the centrally-Planning State, "at the same time as it presents itself as a nation, in order to seek consensus, also organizes and implements capitalist exploitation. On doing so, it sometimes collides with the immediate interests of the local bourgeoisie and of the multinational corporations and is turned into a capitalist-producing State."[20]

The idea of the Entrepreneurial State has doubtless had enormous weight in the orthodoxy of State Planning in Latin America. Precisely the lack of a class of private entrepreneurs capable of dynamically conducting productive expansion and diversification led the State to assume such challenges as its own. The planning of development, driven by the aim of modernizing Latin American societies, lent special importance to the creation of public enterprises for certain areas of the economy whose investment costs could not be covered by the private sector. This brought with it the natural consequence of enormous state participation in strategic areas of the economy. Curiously, the nation's private, entrepreneurial sector, which later undertook sudden anti-Statist attacks, also benefited from this intervention.

Consistent with the paradigm of the Planning State in this context, planning had, as a meta-function, the infusion of an economic rationality analogous to that of the entrepreneurial sector, although on a national scale. The entrepreneurial action of the State could serve, moreover, as a model for private agents. Within this framework the State appeared as the rational head of modernization, and as the example of economic efficiency and of optimized resources. In actuality the terms are inverted, and from diverse political positions it is argued that the State as economic agent ought to learn from the private sector and not vice-versa. If twenty years ago the predominant idea was that the State was situated in the prow of the national development process, from which it oriented private agents, today's prevailing image is exactly the reverse: the State, as economic agent, seems to many in on the stern, or on the poop deck, in the modernization process, where it seems hypertrophied, inefficient, non-actualized, rigid, slow. Contributing to this negative judgment is the fact that the State encountered growing difficulties in the efficient management of public enterprises, dragging along with it a mounting public debt. This further coincides with the fact than in many of the countries of the region dynamic and expansive entrepreneurial classes have been constituted, who regard the size of public enterprises and the state economy as a limitation on their actions. The privatizing wave, as much in ideas as in fact, partially obeys this phenomenon, but it also obeys the greater articulation between private capital within the Latin American countries with transnational capital, which no longer count on the decisive mediation of the State. This mediation is considered by many private agents to be more an obstacle than a vehicle.

The gap between solidity and vulnerability. The archetypal image that the Planning State has wanted to project is that of a solid, stable, effective organism. Nevertheless, the pressures that the State has had to confront, from civil society and from outside, have systematically corroded this image. The gap between solidity and vulnerability wound up bending the paradigmatic image of the State. It did so premised on the following, additional contradictions.

The contradiction provoked *interior-exterior schizophrenia.* The State in Latin America has had to unfold itself in two different personalities: from without and from within. In its role of incorporating the nation into international agreement, politically as much as economically, the State has had to project an image of modernity that coheres with the State in the industrialized world, a State that guarantees internal stability, which is institutionally consolidated and efficient in its actions. But in the internal scope, the State confronts a civil society in a situation of partial or truncated modernization, heterogeneous in its productive structures and in its sociocultural characteristics, towards which it must operate in very distinct languages.

This tendency becomes acute in the present conditions of crisis and external indebtedness. Here, when it looks abroad, the State must tailor itself to the requirements of the regulating financial organisms. When it looks within, it must face a host of social claims which that very same conditioning postponed. The acrobatics of being simultaneously a State that negotiates and guarantees abroad, and a populist State towards within, winds up toppling the acrobatics. A vicious circle is produced in which we currently observe that many of the countries of the region see themselves submerged in the sterile administration of their internal crises and their external pressures. They must deal with the question of how much should the State pledge itself to international financial capitalism as a modern, solvent, and responsible State even as the "recessive" civil society to which it must respond, on the internal front, becomes more heterogeneous, conflictive, and fragmentary. In short, it conducts itself as a State whose external survival requires it to attack the austerity policies that condition the flow of credit towards the country. Yet the more it attacks those policies, the less it can prevent the social fragmentation that the State itself tries to integrate and bring into harmony.

The contradiction provoked by the paradox of the *large but weak* State characterizes the Planning State as it has taken shape in many of countries of the region. In the economic area, the phenomenon of transnationalization makes the regulatory engineering of the State seem increasingly beyond control, given the effects of changes in the global order (in commerce, finance, and production) on internal economies, as well as the increasingly independent power of the national entrepreneurial class in articulation with transnational capital. In politics, the image and claim of the Nation-State, sovereign and autonomous, nevertheless continues to reign. This makes the political image projected by the State seem somehow caricatured by its lack of control over the economic arena.

This tension becomes all the more critical on taking into account the Latin American State's having assumed the historical role of leading actor and agent for modernization. It has been precisely this role, as mega-actor in development, which led to its dynamic of growing absorption in the national budget. This progressive spiral could be maintained while the State suctioned off resources coming from the exportation of raw materials—even up to a couple of decades ago—or international banking during the decade of the 70s, with the multiplied flow of currency coming from the North. But, at present, the situation is exactly the reverse. Not only have the traditional sources of resources for the State been cut off or much reduced, but the State must apportion an important percentage of its liquid capital to servicing the debt. The paradox of a State which is fragile in its capacity to lead, yet broad and dense in its apparatus, disfigures the original image of the Planning State and exacerbates its legitimacy crisis with respect to civil society.

Recapitulating

The preceding reflections enable the visualization of a State in the process of delegitimation. In very divergent lines, neoliberals, communitarians on the left and on the right, and pragmatic politicians have given up on the model of the Planning State. They propose measures, programs, or utopias that rearticulate the itinerary of development from other "centralities" (or "decentralities"). The fact that such diverse political, academic and intellectual postures coincide in seriously questioning the currency and present relevance of the Planning State reveals a certain *sociocultural spirit* of hostility with respect to the proposal of development that said State took as its leading, managing, and articulating axis.

The variety of flanks from which the image of the Planning State is blurred, as mega-actor and meta-actor, allows for the understanding, in its fullest extension, of the crisis of governability so frequently alluded to today, which is often attributed to the processes behind the growing complexity of the social fabric. What's certain is that social complexity and fragmentation have been perceived and assumed with considerable delay. In effect, only their becoming more acute and widely known abroad, through the crisis of the 1980s (and the subsequent adjustment policies, and the greater proliferation of variety in productive processes), forced its consecration as a problematic reality in the sociology of development. But that complexity belongs to the very character of the peripheral and dependent societies which live discontinuous and heterogeneous processes of modernization. If the crisis of governability is explained by the growing complexity of the social fabric, then ungovernability in Latin America unfolds from the historical development model—with its specific mode of articulation between the State and society—throughout most of the countries of the region. The alternatingly authoritarian and democratic governments, like the recurring ruptures of social pacts or interclass agreements promoted by the meta-actor State, show the structural precariousness of the project of the Planning State in past decades: its incapacity for integrating, harmonizing, and conducting without "disrupting functions."

The crisis of the 1980s, like the national economies' growing vulnerability to the financial, productive, and commercial strategies of transnational capital, winds up swamping a boat run aground. The contradictions indicated here are the already constructed bottom, upon which the new scenarios will have their impact. The lack of the State's internal cohesion, like the ambivalence between the national and capitalist State, large and weak, arbitrator and boxing ring, transformer and preserver, are some of the structural aspects from which the crisis of governability can be explained.

What is paradoxical and dramatic in this context is that the State loses legitimacy precisely when it requires the greatest assistance in order to face a crisis of unforeseen proportions. On the one hand its weakening produces a deterioration of image with respect to society. On the other hand, that same deterioration exacerbates its weakness. This vicious circle of the delegitimation of the State (which Habermas perceived a decade before, in the case of the Welfare State in Europe in the 1970s) is particularly critical in the case of the Latin American State in the 1980s. This does not imply, of course, that the forces ought to devote themselves to the restoration of lost legitimacy. It's much more important to ask *how and for whom* the State should be legitimated today, in Latin America. It's certain that growing external vulnerability provoked by the inexorable openings of national economies, added to the state budget crises, rapid productive transformations, and the growing sociocultural fragmentation of societies are conditions that require a strong State, one that is able to convene, to harmonize very heterogeneous social actors, and to rationalize the endowment and use of scarce resources. The State model that could turn out to be more functional in the middle and long range, for dodging the quagmire of underdevelopment, is still unclear.

What enters into play — and into consideration — isn't only a pattern of growth or an economic strategy but, much more than this, a *culture of development* associated with a specific form of articulating the State with civil society. That culture of development, itself induced and disseminated by the Planning State, expresses its fissures in distinct ways: through the crisis of consensus, through the permeability of social sensitivity on the part of the privatizing euphoria and the market offensive, through the sporadic re-sprouting of antidemocratic values in the social fabric and in public institutions, or through the hermetic and atomized withdrawal of distinct social actors. If the crisis of the model of the Planning State is seen as a sociocultural crisis we cannot expect it to resolve itself through technical packaging or the workings of the political will. This doesn't mean that the resolution of the crisis doesn't pose challenges for the government and for planning. On the contrary, what it requires of them is opening up to the sociocultural problem so that they can give the best of themselves. Only through the interrogation of a social project or projects that could turn out to be collectively desirable is it possible to find ways out of the present quagmires. Otherwise, politics runs the risk of turning into bleary-eyed crisis management.

Notes

1   In late capitalism, with the passage from the liberal State to the intervening State, the latter takes on the character of a very powerful economic agent.

2   Enzo Faletto, *Especificidad Estado en America Latina* (Santiago de Chile, División de Desarrollo Social de la CEPAL, 1988), 18.

3   Adolfo Gurrieri, "Vigencia del Estado Planificador en la crisis actual," *Revista de la CEPAL* 31 (Santiago de Chile: 1987), 205.

4   CEPAL-ECLAC had a preponderant role during the 1950s and 1960s in explaining the large-scale strategies of economic development in the region, in giving advice to countries for settling their national plans for development, and in proposing the bases of State planning in Latin America.

5   Marcos Kaplan, "Estado, cultura y ciencia en América Latina," in *Cultura y creación intelectual en América Latina* (México: Siglo XXI, 1984), 103–5.

6   Alfredo Costa-Filho, *Los nuevos retos de la planificación* (Santiago de Chile: ILPES, 1988), 18.

7   José Medina Echevarría's classical text defines the following economic functions of planning: *to stimulate* the economy (privileging certain productive sectors, regulating the consumption and division of labor, etc.); *to distribute* revenue, resources, or potentialities of economic action (regulating credit and taxes); and *to integrate,* ordering or unifying the field of economic activities, bringing harmony to sectors or imposing norms of coherency on the economic system (Medina Echavarría, "Discurso sobre política y planeación," in *La obra de José Medina Echavarría* (Madrid: Ediciones Cultura Hispánica, 1980), 306–307). These wide faculties attributed to planning give an idea of the capacity and weight of planning in the model of the Planning State in Latin America.

8   In present visions planning also covers this function of legitimating power with respect to civil society. Among the functions attributed to it are: providing information to the

government and to society about the most probable future scenarios in which one might be called to live; articulating the whole of public decisions; and providing technical backing to social dialogue between social agents with the aim of strengthening the design and execution of social policies (See the ILPES [Instituto Latinoamericano y del Caribe de Planificación Económica y Social] article, "Planificación para una nueva dinámica económica y social," *Revista de la CEPAL* 31 [Santiago de Chile: 1987]).

9   This last item is the classical criticism of the Welfare State, which argues that the inflation of expectations that the Welfare State provokes in society brings with it a sustained rise in public expenditure, in turn provoking a growing budget deficit, which negatively impacts monetary stability.

10 "Global planning has always been, perhaps, a somewhat utopian concept in a mixed economy. . . . the conditions of the crisis make it even more difficult to carry out the technical aspects of global planning than in more stable epochs. On that account, the application of global planning would intimate delusions of grandeur, although the models of planning might have a heuristic value" (Brian Van Arkadie, "Notas sobre nueve directrices en materia de planificacion," *Revista de la CEPAL* 31 [1987], 36). And in the same key: "Planning is useless, even in market economies; it has an inalienable role to fill within the process of development, but it will continue to be inefficient as long as it is considered a hegemonic task of the State, that decidedly idealized actor, to whom are attributed in a scarcely real fashion, virtues (that it lacks) or irremovable defects (when there is no reason to have them)" (Alfredo Costa-Filho, *Los nuevos retos de la planificación,* 7).

11 Medina Echavarría perceives this tension in a distinct manner. For Medina Echavarría, planning politicizes development in so far as it accentuates the decision making process within its character and in as much as it refers to the rational ordering and total transformation of society, aimed at expanding and sustaining freedom. With this, Medina Echavarría associates planning with Comte and Mannheim respectively, breaking with the more habitual vision of the planner as a technician, and conceding a more political profile to the planner (see José Medina Echavarría, "La planeación en las formas de la racionalidad," in *La obra de José Medina Echavarría,* 377–448).

12 Medina Echavarría, "La planeación en las formas de la racionalidad," 393–403.

13 It's not that the State should be a homogenous block, uniform and molar, where neither internal differences or conflicts are reflected. But the utopia of the Planning State explains the requirement of a highly articulated apparatus which, through being at the height of utopia and utopian goals, should be indivisible and incorruptible.

14 "Class conflicts and those that derive from the process of change not only cross the State but very often it is within the compass of its own apparatus that the political arena is constituted, in which the interests, orientations, and options of the distinct social actors express themselves and compete with one another" (Enzo Faletto, *Especificidad Estado en America Latina,* 26).

15 Useful in this respect is the provocative thought of Agnes Heller: "If cultures are

being pluralized until arriving at the degree of absolute particularization, the question to be posed is whether a meaningful and rational decision making process is still possible. . . . it still isn't clear if pluralization and cultural relativization carry rational politics to extinction, or if they will be the prelude to a more democratic form or forms of political action . . . " (Agnes Heller, "Los movimientos sociales como vehículo de cambio," *Revista Nueva Sociedad* 96 (Caracas: Jul.–Aug. 1988), 44 and 47–48).

16   Osvaldo Sunkel, "Las relaciones centro-periferia y la transnacionalización," *Pensamiento Iberoamericano* 11, (Madrid: Jan.–Feb. 1987), 36–37.

17   Regarding the already paradigmatic case of Peru, two analyses with divergent ideological premises made graphic the ineffectiveness of the State in facing the informal world: José Matos Mar, *Desborde popular y crisis del Estado: el nuevo rostro del Perú en la década de 1980,* Serie Perú Problema 21 (Lima: Instituto de Estudios Peruanos, 1984), and *The Other Path: The Invisible Revolution in the Third World,* Hernando de Soto in collaboration with the Instituto Liberatad y Democracia, foreword by Mario Vargas Llosa (New York: Harper and Row, 1989).

18   Guillermo O'Donnell, "Apuntes para una teoría del Estado," *Revista Mexicana de Sociología* Año XL, Vol. XL No. 4 (Oct.–Dec. 1978), 1195–96.

19   "In the case of Latin America . . . in certain measure it's possible to postulate that the function of 'stimulating capitalism' has corresponded to the State. . . . the proposal of a capitalist society on the part of the State signified that the latter should be formulated for the whole of society, which in fact required that a development plan be explicit. This consequently has to do with a capitalist society that nonetheless incorporated the idea of a Planning State . . ." (Enzo Faletto, *Especificidad Estato en America Latina* 11).

20   Fernando Henrique Cardoso, "El desarrollo en capilla," in *Planificación social en América Latina y el Caribe,* (Santiago de Chile: ILPES / UNICEF, 1981), 38–39.

8 ❊ Is the Social Thinkable without Metanarratives?

Crisis of Intelligibility and Crisis of Organicity

Since the middle of the 1970s the Latin American social scientist has been suffering a crisis of intelligibility and a crisis of organicity. The *crisis of intelligibility* denotes social scientists' progressive difficulty in grasping the growing complexity of social reality by way of previously consecrated cognitive tools. This is evident in the crisis of paradigms in the social sciences, involving the loss of explicative and orienting validity of the three most significant paradigms that governed the practice of the social scientist from the 1950s until the middle of the 1970s: "CEPALism" (the matrix of development discourse), Marxism, and the paradigm of so-called "dependency theorists." The elements that can explain the crisis of these paradigms are multiple, and frequently cited, but the following, very tight synthesis, is worth noting: "The presence of many 'anomalies' that theoretically should not have appeared, or even the emergence of new phenomena that they could not explain (like the paradigm crisis in the natural sciences); the exhaustion of the model of development 'towards within';

the crisis of the populist State (and even more, of the Latin American model of the Planning State); the emergence of authoritarian regimes and their permanence, the processes of growing social division, the growth of the informal sector and of new modalities of marginality, the diversification and deepening of structural heterogeneity, the problems of the processes of democratization."[1] As Heinz Sonntag and Norbert Lechner similarly indicate, from the mid-1970s modernization generated complex processes that the then-available categories could not apprehend. Redefinition and growing differentiation in social structures made for the unfeasibility of a glance that, lacking a globalizing, totalizing rationality, proved incapable of retaining the specificity of these new complexities.[2]

Crisis of organicity refers to the break in the tie between knowledge production and intervention on the real (that is, social change). The political and cultural defeat of the left, and the political and technical defeat of development discourse and its national variants, dismantled the other founding aspect of the architecture of the social sciences in Latin America, namely the organic (or supposedly organic) articulation between the production of knowledge and the radical transformation of society's structures. It's been stated, ad nauseum, that social scientists in Latin America have, almost from the beginning, centered their concerns on the question of social change and of how they, as producers of knowledge, might contribute to the orientation of said change. This social change always had, in the dominant paradigms of production in the social sciences, the sense of modernization of the political, productive, social and cultural structures of the countries of Latin America, although differing in the styles of development, that is, in the contents that modernization should embody with respect to the distribution of political power, economic resources, and social relations. But beginning with the authoritarian offensive and subsequently with the more hegemonic offensive of the neoliberal model, and even more yet with the Welfare State's loss of prestige and still later, with the loud collapse of the socialist models, the Latin American social sciences fell into a conundrum. In postmodern terms, they were left, choked by their metanarratives, caught up in a pitiful self-image, in which the social scientist appears as a mistake of history, or presently impotent.

The present lack of articulation between the *intelligibility of the social* and *intervention on the social* corresponds to increased difficulty in creating a bridge between the re-interpretation of societal processes generated by the new scenarios, and the design of actions organized towards structural change. But in this difficulty, not only do new scenarios intervene, be they international or national, political or cultural. Also evident is a change of the social scientists' perception and stance with regard to Latin American reality. Twenty years ago the sociological exercise was substantially slanted by the conception of a militant science, which made social theory identify with one or another model of political alternative (whether the development model or the socialist one, the two models dearest to development sociology in its times of greatest influence). This was a double-edged sword. On the one hand it made for a tighter and more dynamic relation between theory and practice, between social reflection and political action, between ideological debate and acts of power. On the other hand, however, social reflection was skewed to the extent that the perception of the real often became a subjective construction of reality. At present, the field of the social sciences has slipped into greater academic and political humility. But this replacement of global change projects with the cautious observations of intrasocietal articulations is double-edged as well, serving, on the one side, as an antidote to simplifications that can have lamentable consequences when policies and strategies are derived from them. On the other side, however, it deprives politics of a source of integrating energy which a theoretical production charged with projects for societal transformation previously supplied.

On the other hand, the atomization of knowledge, its multiplication and growing functionality for strictly productive processes, increasingly marginalizes or problematizes "macrosocietal" knowledge or the generation of integrated macrovisions. The tendency of knowledge towards the diversification and acceleration of productive processes pushes in the opposite direction, towards fragmentation, discontinuity, and speed. If sociocultural dispersion and the loss of a oft-noted national cultural identity are added to this, along with the explosion of "microsocietal" logics, the expectation of a totalizing orientation for society can survive only with great difficulty in the discourse of the social scientist.

It is not entirely necessary to allude to the postmodern debate in order to refer to this crisis of intelligibility and of organicity in the field of Latin American social sciences. The theoretical shortcomings and difficulties in insertion currently suffered by the social scientist occur absolutely independent of the texts of Lyotard, Baudrillard or Vattimo. It isn't overly necessary to resort to notions of "multiplicity" in order to maintain a concern with structural heterogeneity. Nor is there much need to resort to "discontinuity" in order to understand truncated modernization, or to "the crisis of metanarratives" in order to feel ourselves lost in facing the lack of large-scale proposals capable of freeing us from underdevelopment and poverty.

There's no need to take an anti-Enlightened stance, to understand the exaggeration with which the Western Enlightenment model of the producer of knowledge was embodied in the model of the Latin American social scientist since the end of World War II. That modern inhabitant of progress, gifted with an almost mythical capacity for deciphering the nature of reason, was then to identify the movement of reason in history, and finally to recognize in that movement, thanks to reason itself, the best direction for the future. And of course, there's no need to resort to the dystopian discourse of disenchantment in order to feel the psychological and even spiritual costs that the pulverization of the image of a possible revolution provoked—a revolution that we were locating in some uncertain future, but towards which the roads were all inevitably leading; a revolution that *as an image* was definitively losing its force for mobilizing the masses, and *as a discourse* was being left without verisimilitude.

What's important here is to show how a mutation of rationalities can impact the means by which a social knowledge has become related to social reality. In this sense, postmodern discourse offers to increase our awareness of this crisis of rationalities of modernity, with the goal of referring a situation of *crisis of intelligibility and organicity of a social knowledge* to a more extensive crisis of rationality.

Planning, Revolution, and the Crisis of Rationalities

In the following pages we will consider certain links between the two most extreme images that strongly influenced Latin American social scientists during the decades of the 1960s and the 1970s. Those images are discovered to be in deep crisis today: the image of state planning and of social revolution. Our analysis will try to refer the crisis of these images and the oft-mentioned *crisis of rationalities* to Latin American modernity. This speculative sequence should not be interpreted as yet another recourse of pro-market ideology in its pretensions towards theoretical and political hegemony. In no way would this be my intention. Quite the opposite: I would like to explore prospective veins in order to reactivate the passions that once upon a time awakened critical thought and the will to utopia. I hope to offer, in this perspective, a distinct comprehension of the connection between the crisis of paradigms and the crisis of organicity in the social sciences, obviating the rhetoric of postmodernity but welcoming the post-modern call to relativize the rationalities that brought legitimacy to the practice of the social scientist.

Planning and revolution constituted the paradigmatic model of the decade's "development from within," which amounted to industrializing modernization and political and social transformation. These were max-imalist notions through which one could most eloquently embody the deliberate intervention of technical and teleological reason in history. It dealt not just with the notions, but with the extreme images for the organicity of social knowledge in the projects of structural change in Latin American societies.

On the side of planning, this could come to be considered the privileged instrument of the large-actor-driver-of-change, which was the Planning State.[3] Within that actor, planning came to constitute an idealized link for the articulation of technical reason with political reason, in order to relate social knowledge with technical intervention from power so that, para-phrasing Hegel, the rational might be more real and the real, more ra-tional. Planning constituted, in this extreme connotation of the term, a palpable example of this organicity of social knowledge in social change. In the extreme image of planning, the social scientist went far back in time, moving from rationalist metaphysical speculation to budgetary and policy programming. As a privileged instrument of modernization and of the dy-namic articulation between the distinct agents of modernization, the plan-ner became a kind of implicit vanguard within the social-constructivist State. Silent, but with much energy, planning was consecrated as a kind of science for the control and orientation of the future. Isn't this, precisely, Enlightenment thinking brought to an extreme?

On the side of the revolution the pretensions were greater, since what was undertaken wasn't to program but to radically subvert an order that constituted a rein on the rationality of history (productive rationality, but above all, social). The revolution symbolized the fusion of the social scien-tist in the struggle for a new order, the definitive embrace of a definitive future. The image of the revolution constituted a motive for the produc-tion of social knowledge. A good part of the literature of development and of sociological and philosophical production, and of production relative to political theory during the 1960s and the beginning of the 1970s, had the revolution as its propelling motif.

Technological rationality, unlike planning, didn't try, in a *minute* man-ner, to construct the future using the present as a point of departure, but rather to interpret the present, in a *thick* manner, using the future as a point of departure.

Situated on opposite poles, both technological rationality and planning fixed the furthest limits within which, in an infinity of combinations and mediations, social scientists "breathed their own air" for unforgettable decades. Both planning and revolution were images weighted down with modern reason: both were permeated with utopianism and enlightenment thinking.[4]

With respect to the crisis of rationalities, this constitutes part of an ongoing discussion in which "critical humanists," on the one hand, and "pragmatic positivists" on the other, have invested much effort: the former in the critique of formal-instrumental rationality, and the latter in the critique of substantive-normative rationality. But despite a lucidity experienced in the critique of these rationalities, the reflection of the modern social sciences was much delayed in considering, in depth, a critique of another two rationalities that were also very much a part of modernity. We'll call them *Enlightenment rationality* and *utopianizing rationality.* The critique of Enlightenment and of utopianism, in its most decided version, arrived all wrapped up in the discourse of postmodernity.

There are three rationalities that I'd want to consider in this context. They all coexist in the cultural architecture of modernity and of modernization: *instrumental rationality,* Enlightenment rationality, and utopianizing rationality. The crisis of these rationalities implies, in the first place, that their political legitimacy is in question, whether because these rationalities show themselves to be less efficacious, or less democratic in the reality of what their apologists initially proclaimed. Secondly, such rationalities lost their rootedness in common sense and in the interpretations that the culture forges with respect to reality and to the changes of reality. Finally, this crisis is also produced because the conflicts between these rationalities (between instrumental reason and utopianizing reason, between Enlightenment reason and instrumental reason, between means and ends) wind up relativizing and even reciprocally neutralizing the mobilizing capacity that those paradigms exercise over collective action.

The practice of the planning and discourse of revolution embodied the adduced rationalities with special force. In the basic structure of the mentality of the planner and the revolutionary, instrumentalism, enlightenment thinking, and utopianism coexist, often without the planner or revolutionary ever perceiving themselves to be situated at the intersection of these three rationalities. Thus my interest in further developing these connections.

Instrumental Reason, Planning, and Revolution

Instrumental rationality is at the basis of the technical development that characterizes the processes of modernization. It is founded in the criteria of effectiveness and productivity. In the economic realm it is associated with the maximalization of utilities. In the political realm, it is associated with the rationalization of power and the 'added' conduct of social actors.

Planning is crossed by instrumental rationality from its very basis. In the case of Latin American societies, the apogee of planning, above all from the beginnings of the 1960s, follows from the conviction that it's possible to rationalize the economic management of society with the goal of optimizing the use of resources, to increase productivity and to transform the productive sphere with an eye to maximalizing results. At the same time, conventional planning exhibits a markedly economic bias, which implies that its ends are nothing but means: increasing profit, multiplying productivity, and diversifying production.

From the side of revolutionary discourse, the presence of instrumental reason is more ambiguous. On the one hand, there's no doubt that the exercise of power in the real experiences of socialist States reveals an exhaustive and functional rationalization of political relations. Instrumentality has been undeniable there, expressed in the bureacratization of the mediations between State and society, and in the subjection of state action to a logic of political effectiveness. The presence of an instrumental logic is also clear in the Leninist discourse that many revolutionary leftist parties engage from their very origins, and that go on to characterize the vertical relations between their leadership and base members. This modality of "organic" militancy that characterized the parties of the left over a long period of time in Latin America, and into which many progressive intellectuals also entered, was permeated by instrumental rationality.

But revolutionary discourse was, on the other hand, also interwoven with elements that cannot be considered subordinate to a technical rationality. Revolutionary mysticism, the sacrificial dimension in the extreme image of the militant of the revolution, the epic connotations in the rhetoric of radical change, the unreality of many of the strategies and proposals impelled from the supposedly educated, well-read leftists of our countries: all these are elements that doubtless exceed any kind of instrumental rationality.

The critique of instrumental reason derives from various theoretical and ideological sources. One could trace those sources, in the Weberian radiography of modern, formal rationality and in the critique of instrumental reason undertaken by T. A. Adorno and Max Horkheimer, from the Frankfurt School. Later, these critics have been refitted and reformulated from political theory as well as from the sociology of development.

Within this framework, normative planning has been questioned for its tendency to dissolve "the great policy" in social engineering, and by the consequent omission of the question for the meaning of modernization directed from the State. The orthodox discourse of the socialist revolution has also been questioned in its instrumental dimension, especially by the tendency to assume, acritically, an instrumental logic in the struggle for power.

The literature of development already shows in this field an important stockpile in a divergent sense. The contributions made in order to conceive alternative styles of development—centered on quality of life, the democratization of social relations, the communitarian ethic or environment equilibrium—all reveal an effort to overcome the technicological bias in the culture of development. The diverse contributions have in common the questioning of modern formal-instrumental reason, a questioning which functions in them as a kind of initial effort, and which subsequently turns to query the ends, ruling values, and orienting utopias of development. It moves on to query, as well, the consistency of procedures with ends, and of felt necessities with the planning of necessities. The emphasis with which said reflections support other logics woven through the social fabric—the logics of solidarity, sacrifice, communication, redistribution—is born from this return to ends and values in discussions of development.

But the critique of the instrumental bias of planning, of the "Leninist" discourse of the revolution or of the agenda for the construction of economies of centralized planning, not only derives from this new reading of development where the disenchanted come together from the militant left, from development discourse, and from progressive humanism in order to recycle their hopes and their proposals. There is also a sharp critique from liberalism, much more widely disseminated by the academic sphere, the most influential political circles, and by the mass media. The emphasis of liberal critique of instrumental reason promoted by the Planning State, be it the Welfare State or the Socialist State, is, nevertheless, symmetrically opposed: it does not object to the surplus engineering in the rationalization imposed by state planning. Quite the contrary: the liberal critique objects to ineffectiveness, in a line whereby neoliberals affirm that planning should occur "spontaneously" from the market, rather than from the State, and that processes of economic rationalization should be articulated from the market, rather than the State, if instrumental reason is to operate with greater effectiveness. In other words, would-be private economic agents, rather than the agents of the state apparatus, would allow for the dissemination of this rationality in distinct spheres of activity.

Hayek has formulated the most widely known argument in this sense, and his argument has been exhaustively repeated by the apostles of monetarism in Latin America. According to Hayek, the quantity of information and of variables to consider in economic management is of such magnitude that one cannot expect a reduced group of persons to appropriate the faculty of conducting the economy of a country and to claim to do so while optimizing the yield of the factors and the coordination of the activities. In consequence, and given that said information is found disseminated between the dispersed mass of private economic agents, only the signals of the market have a regulatory effectiveness capable of rationalizing the system as a whole. In this way, the neoliberal critique questions not a kind of instrumental rationality but rather, the place — or agent — from which said rationality is formulated and promoted. With this, the critique attacks both planning and socialism, arguing that both resort to a kind of rationalization of productive factors that deny the very effectiveness that they claim to impel.

The neoliberal critique holds that there is a basic contradiction in the combination of economic rationalization with redistributive policies (a combination that is at the very marrow of the planner's discourse and of socialism in general). According to this argument, social redistribution muddies the rules of the game of the market and in so doing enters into the deployment of rational economic behaviors, restricting entrepreneurial freedom and producing grave distortions in the signals of the economy. So the redistribution of social wealth would attack the principle of efficient rationality, and could only be consistent with economic rationality in special circumstances in which it would be necessary to reactivate the economy by way of energetic stimulation of consumption. But it's an obstacle to said rationality when it limits the power of gain on the part of private agents or when it unleashes inflationary processes in which investment becomes risky and much more uncertain.

Between the critique of the instrumental rationality of state planning, and the orthodoxy of the left formulated by the paladins of alternative development, and the critique that the neoliberals propose, there exist coincidences and important differences. Both coincide in indicating that the Planning State, be it capitalist or socialist, cannot attempt to rationalize from the above social behaviors in a uniform, homogenous manner. Both coincide in emphasizing the relative autonomy that civil society should enjoy, with regard to the State. They both coincide, finally, in the need to stimulate creativity and individual as well as group initiatives, and suggest that such potentialities not see themselves neutralized or coopted by state centrality. But while neoliberalism and the present expansive tendency of the market economies do not renounce, but rather redouble their enthusiasm for the instrumental rationality of economic agents and social relations, the "alternativist" position is especially critical in this respect. While neoliberalism is reluctant to engage redistributive policies, alternativism proposes that all desirable development proceeds from processes of exhaustive redistribution of socially produced resources. While neoliberalism supports the autonomy of civil society by way of the market, alternativism ties together autonomy and communitarian participation, local development and/or the ties of solidarity within spaces on the micro-scale. These differences become difficult to reconcile upon passing from the critique of instrumentality to proposals for alternative forms of development.

Enlightened Reason, Planning, and Revolution

The critique of enlightened reason has also been formulated from various ideological stances. Postmodernists on the right and on the left have strongly questioned it, concentrating its critical arsenal on objecting to the metaphysics of progress, the mystification of the leading vanguard, and the euphoria of integrating modernization.[5]

With regard to the critique of the notion of progress—an idea at the core of Enlightenment modernity—it is argued that history does not march forward and upwards, and that its discontinuous and multidirectional character redounds with considerable margins of uncertainty regarding the future. Since history does not appear to be regulated by an internal, unmistakable kind of rationality, its unfolding is unforeseen as being provisional at best. From this perspective, to think of knowing the internal reason of history — assuming that there is one — and from there to scientifically regulate society, economy, and culture, appears as a megalomaniac delusion, with totalitarian consequences.

This bears on the demystification of the avant-gardes. If history has no rational direction, this shows the lack of legitimacy for the aspiration of a group that adjudicates in itself *the* objective interpretation of history, and with this as a base, arrogates to itself the right, globally, to formulate norms. Neither the educational elite, nor science, nor the State can, in consequence, aspire to establish totalizing orientations. With the erosion of the image of progress and of certainty regarding an underlying reason in history, the avant-garde assumes the face of the despot.

The conventional image of revolution as much as the dominant style of planning are thus seen as substantially deligitimated. In its theoretical conception as in its historical reality, planning has been a meeting point between science and the State. It supposes rational historicity at the same time as it supposes the capacity to craft said rationality from a plan designed and brought about by a group in which expertise and power are condensed. If one does not socially recognize a clear and positive historical directionality, and if one does not admit the capacity of a restricted group "to read" the present scientifically and to orient it effectively towards the future, then it would be difficult to appropriate legitimacy to the normative planning that underlies the Planning State. What appears as illusory in this new "politico-cultural temper" is the hypostatic conception of the State, understood as a kind of "Hegelian synthesis" which, independent of the vicissitudes of contingency, always constitutes the highest moment of the rationality of history and the most suitable management of society. At these heights it's difficult to think of the present Latin American State as the harmonic totalizer of social interests.

The image of socialist revolution has also received quite a beating in its Enlightenment matrix for being evidenced in the history of the *reversibility* of socialism. Of course, in Latin America, from the beginnings of the 1960s, the overthrow of progressive governments by right wing military coups already made problematic, from the perspective of the struggle for power, the supposed historical inevitability of the revolution. Furthermore, from the middle of the 1970s, the social sciences had to seriously propose up to what point that limiting image of a socialist revolution, with the characteristics attributed to it from the Cuban Revolution, could operate as an intellectual superego (as much in terms of the possible as well as of the desirable). But it was with the abrupt fall of the socialist systems in the East, at the end of the 1980s, that the narcissist image of a revolution from the west received its bloodiest blow. From this historical inflection it became unlikely, in practice, to associate *that* revolution with progress, with the freeing of human potentials, or with the optimal development of productive forces. The failures were so patently revealed that it was no longer possible to attribute the regressive image of socialism to the capitalist press. The revolution remained without the support of reason in history.

The myth of integrating modernization also collapsed under its own weight, for that myth is understood as deriving from the modern myth of progress. Confidence in rationality and historical continuity could not be more marked than in the vision of integrating modernization that emanates from the Planning State, which that State proposes to society as a natural itinerary. What is in doubt here is the idea that following the compass of the times *necessarily* requires carrying out occupations of growing productivity, promoting progressive grades of formal education and massively incorporating a "literate" sensibility to the population. The educational-industrialist utopia that forms the symbolic substratum of the Planning State defines the ultimate objectives of development as based on an ideal, homogenous society with growing productivity. Within this framework, the task that the Planning State assumes with regard to its own historical project does not substantially differ from the Enlightenment project that underlies modernity: under an articulated direction, to integrate the process of accumulating knowledge, the development of productive forces, and the socio-political order.[6]

In this way, the crisis of Enlightenment reason flows into the questioning of the theoretical-ideological models that were so very influential during the 1960s in the region. Despite expressing opposing political engagements at the time, capitalist development discourse, like state-centered socialism, referred back to a model of normative planning, whether for mixed economies or for state economies, where the plan represented the highest possible degree of rationalization of historical directionality. Curiously, it has been a certain kind of postmodern liberalism that has induced a retrospective reading of our history, which disenchanted leftists to some degree share, and in which the development discourse as well as the socialism of the 1960s are siblings on the same branch of the family tree. This shows us where the Planning State gravitates when the political past of our countries is reconstructed. Because what can 1960s-style development discourse and socialism unequivocally share, if not the axiomatic approval of the Planning State? Would it not be in the use of central planning, as a means for "molding" society according to the intentions of reason, where development discourse and socialism can be considered part of the same world-vision, and not as irreconcilable opponents? Do they not both reproduce the Enlightenment task of social emancipation, which development discourse defines as modernization and emancipation with respect to the "traditional" or "primitive" forms of social reproduction, and which socialism defines as emancipation with respect to international capital — imperialism — or with respect to the oppressive relations of production? And wouldn't the role of the Planning State be crucial in whichever of the two images of social emancipation — whether to overcome technical delay, or to overcome domination — to the point that in both positions this historical reason only becomes real from the moment that it is embodied in the Planning State's power to regulate society?

The critique of development discourse and of socialism that this postmodern liberalism infers from its critique of Enlightenment reason is nonetheless closely bound up with pro-market ideology, which has been increasingly on the offensive in all latitudes over the course of the last decade. This mixture of anti-Enlightenment and anti-State thinking can be summarized as a critique of the transformational function of politics (except when aimed at privatization and economic deregulation), and as a critique of state intervention in regulating economic relations.

But another qualification that the image of socialist revolution or the practice of State planning both face, which also derives from the anti-Enlightenment critique, is the one formulated from the culturalist perspective and from currents of democratic political theory presently in vogue. In the first case — the culturalist perspective — the referents of planning and revolution are reproached for their ethnocentric bias. It is argued that these referents do one of the following: they may look to the industrial world, in a development style and set of expectations that they seek to impose on developing countries, in a model "from above onto below." Or, they may take as a model an emancipatory ideal belonging to European modernity, a model incapable of taking up the cultural identity of Latin American peoples. In this way, the critique of Enlightenment reason is translated into the critique of the reductionist imposition of the exogenously induced pattern of development or redemption of history. In the second instance — the perspective of a revalorization of democracy — the exhaustive reach of the Planning State, or of the eventual socialist State, is questioned, in turn valorizing the relative autonomy of civil society and a sociopolitical order based in a wide social agreement. In this agreed upon order, much noted "historical directionality" would not turn out to be monopolistically concocted from the central power constituted by the planners and political agents of the revolution. Rather, that "historical directionality" would result from the processes of negotiation and consensus among multiple social actors.

From this optic, the utopia of the socialist revolution or of the Planning State (as the axis and driver of the model of modernization) seems incompatible with a social democracy that encourages the proliferation and expression of diverse logics expressed in the social fabric, which have been called the logics of social movements. Likewise, the invocation of social creativity and diversity do not aim to strengthen the market against the State, but to call attention to social complexity, to the variety of actors and sociocultural costs that the enterprise of homogenizing modernization drags after it.

In synthesis, the archetypal images underlying planning and revolution lead into the mystification of progress, of the rational avant-garde, and of integrating modernization to such a point that if we were to subtract any one of these three foundations for the organicity of social knowledge, that knowledge would tend to disappear from the epistemological horizon. These foundations are as much normative as they are epistemological. They are normative in that the idea or image of revolution or planning challenges obligates the social scientist to produce knowledge that can foment and make viable the practice of planning or of a possible revolution. These foundations are epistemological in that an ideal construction (such as the former ideals of the revolution or of planning) offers positionality and meaning to the social scientist's research.

Utopianizing Reason, Planning, and Revolution

The outbreak of economic crisis at the beginning of the 1980s, and the collapse of socialism facing the alternative of the market at the end of the 1980s, put an inflexible ceiling on development and social change as these had been conceived, both historically and from the optic of theories of social change, in Latin America. An inevitable consequence of this objective and exogenous limit imposed by the crises has been the withdrawal of utopianizing reason,[7] since such reason requires, for its own deployment, an open horizon. But here too the economic crisis and the defeat of socialism do no more than make explicit a utopian image that was born condemned by its own excess. Because these two paradigmatic images combine two ideals that are not easily harmonized: a technical idea of maximum development of the productive forces and a sociopolitical ideal of construction of civil society by the State.

What constitutes this juxtaposition between technical and sociopolitical ideals, between instrumentalism and utopianism? In the model of the Planning State, technical reason presupposes that *utopia is only worth thinking about if it's plannable* — that is, if one can sketch out a technically viable itinerary for conducting the present towards that utopian construction. In this way, in the model of development ruled by the Planning State, the planning of utopia combines or mingles with the utopia of planning — that is, with the conviction that planning is more apt to be attained if it can be universalized. So that in the practice of normative planning, what's lacking is the exhaustibility of the instrumental handling of development: the desirable is the full correspondence between the plan — its objectives, its duration — and its effective crystallization. Utopia is the reality regulated by the judgment of productive reason, by the horizon of economic modernization, by intersectorial balances and the improvement reflected in combined economic indicators.[8]

The critique of utopian reason also has two divergent ideological-theoretic strains. On the one hand, there is an objection to the coercive strength that the utopian construction can exercise over reality. In this argument, the utopian referent operates creating norms and directing the present, closing off perspectives and subjecting it to the straightjacket of utopia. On the other hand, the critique of utopian reason is wielded from resurrected realism or political pragmatism, indicating that utopian thought distorts and simplifies the conflicts that really exist, that it sidesteps the relation of real forces and agents, and winds up confusing desires with facts. We shall see, further on and with greater detail, these two flanks of attack on utopian rationality that can be applied as much to the idea of revolution as to the discourse of the normative planner.

The critique of *utopian determinism* has been formulated by neoliberal thinkers, originally inspired in Karl Popper's critique of Plato, Hegel, and socialism in general. This line of reasoning argues that a normatively proposed model, that therefore aspires to regulate from an ends defined as valid for everyone by the global historical directionality, is incompatible with the image of an "open" society — understanding, with this term, a society free to choose and rectify its own destiny, or to permit as many destinies as there are people composing it. This critique of the utopian construct tends to be joined with a critique of statism. It's not surprising that Popper has chosen to attack the statist utopias of Plato and Hegelianism of the Left.

This attack on utopia is easily extended to planning and to the idea of revolution, and it's no accident that in neoliberal discourse the two enjoy so little favor. Planning and revolution are seen as forms of "exercising power over the future," which is exactly how Popper and his intellectual heirs look at the utopian construct. Consequently, the image of the Planning State or of revolutionary power would produce such reactions in the utopian-aversive neoliberal sensibility, reactions that likewise are notoriously extended into the discursive field of postmodernism. Development driven from the top down, by a group, like development driven by the Planning State or by the revolutionary program, would be, from its very formulation, a menace to the open society. The rational utopia that underlies the similar image of the State, according to which the latter embodies an optimizing rationality, would be inexorable as well, and would then constitute the first step towards the coming of a totalitarian order hyper-regulated by a power that, in its turn, indefinitely perpetuates its regulation.

This warning could have paranoid connotations and could serve as an argument for liberal crusades which in themselves sometimes acquire totalitarian streaks. But there's no reason, on this account, to engage in denial or make light of the matter. What neoliberal fears posit for democratic thought in general and above all in countries of peripheral-dependence capitalism, is the challenge of rethinking the image — or the model — of the State as Conductor so that it opens its utopian horizon to multiple rationalities, instead of or preceding rationalities in communications, eudaemonics, solidarities, fraternity, and/or participation. Only by relativizing utopian reason (as a form of *utopianizing reductionism,* be it formalist or finalist) is it possible to undermine the foundations of the fears of neoliberals and postmoderns. This requires a profound revision of the culture of modernization, for this very culture has served as symbolic substratum making up the image of the Planning State.

The second critique of utopian reason does not question the utopian exercise as such. Rather, it seeks to specify its political and epistemological functions. What this critique objects to are the utopia's pretensions to feasibility and the distortions that said pretensions generate in the perception of the existing order. Such an objection does not necessarily have a defined political character. It has been formulated by intellectuals situated in very diverse points of the ideological spectrum, in distinct ways and with diverse emphases.

In the political aspect, the critique in question is tied to the recent resurgence of political realism. From this position, the maximalist tendency is questioned with every intention of practicing politics departing from utopia. Similar maximalism is liable to flow into a kind of political lack of realism that winds up frustrating effective attempts towards structural change in society. Under this perspective, utopianism is associated with an excessive ideologization suffered by the left in past decades, where the maximalist positions or the symbolic referent of the revolution will have underestimated the objective weight of the social forces that have been opposed — and are opposed — to the proposals for radical change.

The epistemological critique questions the confusion that utopian reason generates when it wants to perceive present reality as only a necessary moment in the road towards the realization of utopia. Reality then moves on to be "read" as a pending ideal, which tends to slant many aspects and actors that compose the real system and that don't necessarily march in line towards the utopian city. Utopianism reissues, in a mundane version, the old concept of Providence that lived on until the rationalist megalomania of Hegel. From this illusion, once again, all of the real seems rational and all of the rational seems capable of being realized.

Facing this distortion of utopian reason, epistemological criticism holds that the utopian construction ought, as a purpose, to serve as a reference of intelligibility, that is, to contrast objective limitations and restrained potentialities with a utopian ideal of limitations overcome and of freed potentialities. Utopia would then be a contrasting reference for comprehending a specified reality, and a horizon of reference allowing for the orientation of actions in a directionality that the utopia itself would indicate as desirable. But it is crucial to delimit this methodological function of utopia and not to fall into a type of idealization in which the differences between ideal construction and real world are erased. Said confusion attributes to utopia an ontological quality that it does not possess.

This political and epistemological crisis is as applicable to the discourse of the revolution as to the discourse underlying planning. One could think, for example, that the multiple functions adjudicated to the Planning State, as meta-actor and as mega-actor, and as great societal conductor and articulator, derive from the assumption of a flexible social reality, capable of being harmonized from above, and of a progressive flow of resources towards the State.[9] The idea that one could conjugate economic development with profound transformations of the social structures, and all of this with a degree of conflict sufficiently tenuous so that the State would be able to arbitrate without substantial mishaps, does not seem consistent with a realistic analysis of Latin American societies. This utopian maximalism that would animate the enterprise of the Planning State also worked, with very different contents and programs, in the other enterprises that awakened such adhesion among many intellectuals and politicians in the 1960s: the socialist revolution.

With respect to the confused ontological status of utopia, it suffices to remember that the socialist revolution and normative planning were never perceived as utopian constructs (at least, not during the height of the idea and its application). Rather, they were seen as programs designed in accordance with the reason of history. Such programs were, in both cases, an itinerary of rationalization of the society by the State, with a more technical slant in the case of planning, and a more teleological one in the case of the revolution. In both cases, political power was the trustee.

But also, in both cases, the transit of the ideal construct to action occurred with minimal mediation on the part of reality. The limits between the ideal construct and perception of reality became vague and ambiguous. With the apogee of planning unleashed in 1961 under the Alliance for Progress, national plans for development not only appeared as the bridge between the possible and the desirable. From its scrupulous instrumental rationality, it also depicted a reality to be sculpted by the planner's utopia. Time, along with the interests of some and the power of others, showed that reality was neither so docile or so lineal.

In the field of image production of the revolution, the appeal to the political will was much more explicit than in that of planning. At the same time, however, the image of the revolution was swathed in an epic clothing that wound up, in many cases, avoiding the real correlation of political forces. That the bloody military coups had taken the intellectuals and left wing parties by surprise reveals this lack of political realism for which the left wing was so often blamed afterwards. The epic character assigned to the revolutionary process, and the mythification of the agent (be it the militant, the people, the worker, or the guerilla of the revolution) were the elements of utopianization in apologists for radical social change.

How much did the social sciences contribute to these errors of perception and to these biases in intelligibility? In what measure did the production of social knowledge construct, and in what measure did it interpret, those enlightened and utopianizing myths with which normative planning and the theorists of the revolution operated? To what point did this maximalism of the normative planner (to control exhaustively the process of development) and of the revolutionary intellectual (to transform exhaustively the relations between the actors of development) form part of the social scientist's imagination during decades that were most constitutive of Latin American social science? In what measure, finally, did these ideal types serve as motives and horizons of reference for the practice of research, reflection, and teaching in the field of the Latin American social scientist until the middle of the 1970s? And if all this had to find a positive response, at least in a considerable proportion: how much of this remains at present, how much is dragged against the current of disenchantment and of self-criticism, how much is transformed into new utopias and new models of "negotiation" between science and power? In the heat of such disenchantments and reformulations, it isn't easy to have any kind of clarity on these points.

New Sensibilities Facing the Crisis of Rationalities

A cartography of these rationalities in crisis should contribute to a different perception of the crisis in which the social sciences have had to endure for more than a decade in Latin America. If the images that would sustain a fully self-justified identity for the social scientist have been systematically knocked down prior to constructing new images, it would be best to ask in what measure they might have a chance of proposing, as a source of legitimation for the Latin American social scientist, alternative images that might well be born from the same trunk of rationalities. Perhaps it's best, today, to hope, to observe, to maintain a low profile in the respective fields of activity, and to let the discourse of history go on a bit, in order to see if a pendular movement returns the social sciences to the urgent necessity of consecrating great rationalities and historical directionalities.

The current options seem to point towards new mediations between the social scientist and his or her object, or between knowledge and reality. A bit of Enlightenment and utopianism might ward off the tendency towards excessive functionalism and pragmatism that threatens to co-opt the production of the social scientists. A bit of Enlightenment or utopianism might limit the a-critical apologies made in defense of the functions of the market. It might be possible to widen the concept of rationality to the scope of the cultural self-production of society, to new life strategies, to the irreducible mestizo that underlies and survives in Latin America. It could be possible speak in the plural, in perspectives, in simulacra, or in alternative scenarios, and to be more humble in the transmission of knowledges, but more adventurous in experimenting with knowledges. To carry the value of pluralism from the political to the epistemological option, to be pluralist as social scientists. To modify the form as much as the contents, personal attitude as much as the object. To become, for a while, the very object of research, to become fully aware of one's own disenchantment and perplexity, and that of peers and neighbors. To discard nothing as irrational or irrelevant. To examine from close up the cultural shades and profiles, the qualities of sensitivity and of personality, in ways that a planner or scientist of the revolution never imagined doing.

The social sciences can't revive a corpse. If a cultural death exists in society and it's impossible, then, in a given moment, to produce fresh and renewed images of itself, one can't expect the social sciences to ward off the dominant note of indifference towards the future or the tendency to renounce large-scale, collective projects. Social scientists have always been creative as interpreters of the real movement of the society, or of the multiple movements of social reality. For the raw material of what they would work out, however, they require the cultural energies that society itself is capable of generating. If today those energies remain opaque or refracted, the social scientist would have to develop a new clinical eye, to practice with his or her own disenchanted or desolated body, and from there to incite the social imagination towards the hope of a new swing of the pendulum. To be alert, to avoid that typical discursive obesity of those who have little to really propose, to empathize with what's coming in order to be able to become fully aware of new rationalities. To maintain a certain vitalism and, at the same time, this critical and revealing gaze in which the best of modern humanism survives.

With all this, I don't want to fall into the recipe of easy ways out of the postmodern discourse. I am not talking, here, about celebrating disenchantment, or about proclaiming that finally the social sciences have been freed from the chains of Reason, Logos, and from the commitment both to history and to the end of history. Nor do I want to reduce ethical problems to an ambiguous aesthetic glance, or practical problems to utterly individual options. I do not want to soften the social and structural heterogeneity under the gallant epithet of "plasticity."

Nor do I believe that the critique of historical directionality, and above all of present history, should prevail towards the negation of all directionality capable of conferring meaning and direction to society as a whole. What should indeed be relativized, in this weakening of large-scale, future projects, with regard to the challenge of modernization, is the prevailing style of development, as a style that takes the present condition of the metropolis, or of industrialized societies, as its norm for the future.

But if the social sciences want to go beyond the ritual of exegesis within the cloistered walls of the university, if they want to break with the atomized and taxonimized mold of the practice of knowledge in the research centers, if they want to transcend the casuistry towards some link where casuistry no longer has that amorphically descriptive mold in which it finds itself encapsulated, if they want to go a little bit beyond the technical assessments for ministers and cabinet members, a bit beyond political publicity and opinion polls, a bit beyond elegant marketing and the technocrat's life in international organizations, if they want to go a bit beyond all these substitutional or chancy forms of articulation between science and social life, social science will have to let itself be a little contaminated by the new sensitivities proclaimed in postmodern discourse. Without this having to lead into a *cool* look at the problems that, like all the big social problems in Latin America, are really boiling.

Maybe this contamination will sharpen the spirit of the social scientist and allow for a rediscovery of new incipient tendencies in which there are new rationalities and utopias in the process of gestation. These might be utopias attributed to the new social movements, with their respect for diversity, their will to local autonomy, their vocation for solidarity. These might be the utopias that privilege the cultural specificity of Latin America and from there seek to think about more authentic ways of living together. It might be the more institutionalist utopia that potentially dwells in the new democracies, understood as the promise of greater political participation, wider citizen action, wider citizenship. They might be new forms coming from the field of art, intellectual production or survival strategies. And planning or revolution would no longer be the extremes within which the legitimated self-image of the social scientist would be sketched. Others will come, just as they have come, over recent years: community organizer, arts critic, telluric metaphysician, or market socialist.

It's worth it, for now, this odd combination of prudence and adventurousness, this opening up of perspectives, this experimentation in knowing, this heterodoxy in the expectation of new signs.

Notes

1   Jorge Vergara, "Crisis y transformaciones de las ciencias sociales latinoamericanas," a paper presented to the IX Seminar of the Commission for Epistemology and Politics in CLACSO (Santiago de Chile, November 28–29, 1991), 5. Parentheses added.

2   "The celebrated 'paradigm crisis' sprung from the recognition of its inability to decipher and explain in a global form a reality turned extraordinarily complex" (Heinz Sonntag, *El estado de arte en las ciencias sociales latinoamericanos,* [Caracas, 1991], 11). See also Norbert Lechner, *Los desafíos de las ciencias sociales en América Latina* (Santiago de Chile: FLACSO, 1988), which similarly stresses the dissolving impact of increasing social complexity in the "historical" paradigms of the Latin American social sciences.

3   Understood as the maximalist extension with which it was incorporated into the political imagination, up to the middle of the 1960s: as Demiurge State, meta-actor, conductor of industrializing modernization, impartial arbiter of social conflicts and great political totalizer.

4   But it's also certain that the revolution, as the hope and image of a distinct future, was also clothed in many images that weren't modern, or even less "rational": messianism, fundamentalism, providentialism, and salvationism were always present in the discourses and revolutionary sentiments in Latin America.

5   In this respect, a more detailed analysis can be consulted in this book's chapter on the postmodern debate.

6   The modernization that since the end of World War II assumes a defined profile in Latin America "is inferred from those economic and social transformations that took place in some countries of Latin America as a consequence of the processes of dependent industrialization after the Second World War. This is the sense in which we should understand modernization as a series of changes that, beyond the purely economic, encompassed the cultural realm and were ideologically expressed in the conviction that the 'history' of the countries of the continent advanced in a progressive direction towards 'higher stages.' This modernizing vision branched outward in turn, in two strains: one that we here will call *developmentalist* and another that we'll call, provisionally, *revolutionary*" (Fernando Mires, "Continuidad y ruptura en el discurso político," *Revista Nueva Sociedad* 91 [Caracas: Sept./Oct. 1987], 129).

7   "Utopianizing reason," not "Utopian reason," since the latter indicates that reason itself is a utopia, and not a producer of utopias. The term "*utopianizing* reason," in turn, denotes this productive character of reason, which in this case turns out to be very pertinent to explicate.

8   The pretension that normative planning, conceived as instrumentalist utopia, could be

considered as a form of subsuming political conflicts in formal structures. Within this framework, planning found itself with the problem that arises as a "strategic" attribute of a State in the process of historical formalization (a process never completely achieved). As a consequence, it's impossible to separate the crisis of legitimacy in planning from the crisis of the State, especially from the crisis of the State as an ideal construction.

9 For a more exhaustive analysis of the utopia of the Planning State, see the chapter titled "Crisis of Legitimacy in the Planning State," included in this book.

9 ❀ Utopia against Crisis, or How to Awake from a Long Insomnia

Crisis and Utopian Thought

Today as never before, the nations of Latin America coincide in institutionalizing and promoting democratic politics. For the first time in the republican era, all the countries of the region are reckoning on popularly elected governments. This consecration of democracy takes place, symptomatically, at the same historical period when great utopias have lost legitimacy, utopias that in preceding decades fed the Latin American political imagination. At the same time as institutions are being democratized, the politicians are reducing their ambitions. Paradoxically, the gain in stability is matched by a loss of mobilizing force.

This loss of utopic force runs the risk of reducing politics to its institutional, bureaucratic, and technocratic dimensions. It becomes urgent, then, to seek out and question new mobilizing utopias, so that political practice can propose substantive projects. These new utopias, in distinction to the preceding ones, should be formulated in order to recreate the future, rather than to nail it down. The following questions arise, then:

how to plan for open utopias, which for all their openness will not be indeterminate? How to articulate utopic construction with political practice so that the latter comes to be inscribed in the universe of collective signs without its becoming, on this account, something that overdetermines its horizon of possibilities?

The integrating visions of modernity have exploded into multiple, low profile strategies in which the dream of the transformed and redeemed community no longer counts. The global economic recomposition and total demystification of real socialisms have left modernity bereft of mass dreams. The masses are less and less thought of as effervescent, mobilized, challenging. The tendency towards collective resignation, together with the administrative and pragmatic biases of politics, have created a situation that could be defined as a crisis of utopian thinking.

The positive image of the postwar period depended on the fact that each country would find plenty of meaning in the elaboration of collective projects or development styles founded in clear rules and goals. There now appears, by way of contrast, the image of governments forced to administer a crisis that they have not chosen and that determines them from the very onset. We become, progressively, "sleepwalking administrators of a crisis that we intuit as impossible to resolve by our own means. This somnambulant state, in which the crisis of utopia flows out into us, is manifest in many faces: defeatism, demobilization, lack of will power, exacerbated individualism, fear, anguish, cynicism."[1] The market economy's aspirations to assert hegemony over reflection on the future of development have sought to strip legitimacy from the utopias that, during the preceding decades, animated politics and planning in our countries. The only ones to resist this, with their customary viscosity, were some closed-off utopic tales that were entrenched in local spaces, in raving millenalianism or in hermetic cultural identities.

Utopic thought doesn't have the strength to push back the crisis. It nonetheless has the mobilizing effect of shaking up the gregarious skepticism that has spread out under the eaves of the crisis. If utopia possesses, by definition, a certain impossible character, its contrasting effect allows one to unmask the irrationality of the situation from which one imagines utopias. To conceptualize utopias can be none other than to express collective desires for collective unrealities. Yet its very expression is, under regressive circumstances, a critical event.

In the pages that follow, we will return to fathom the folds of utopia and its architecture of origin, with the intention of recuperating speculative elements that are negated today by the anti-utopian ebb and tide. With this battery charged we will return, in the concluding pages of this chapter, to the sense and meaning of utopic thinking in Latin America.

Utopia and Critical Function

Etymologically speaking, utopia is nowhere. Ontologically speaking, it's a real impossibility, an absent presence, the unlocatable that makes our location easier. It's the eye that watches from the imagination, the desire that lies in wait, the hope that defends.

A look at the most widely known classical utopias, from Plato to Francis Bacon, shows that the relation between utopic construction and reality tends to follow a common pattern — that is, that utopia always supposes a critique and questioning of the existing order. Thomas More's *Utopia*, published for the first time in around 1516, embodies the tension between political-instrumental reason and the incipient development of commercial capitalism in the Old World on the one hand, and, on the other, expectations regarding the New World as a communitarian paradise. Thomas More devotes the first part of his *Utopia* to expounding the disastrous consequences of that exalted modernization: the enclosure of the common lands with the consequent expulsion of great masses of peasants and the economic polarization brought about by commercial capitalism in the Renaissance. Utopia is the critique and negation of private property and of the demoralized face of politics: " 'Till property is taken away there can be no equitable or just distribution of things, nor can the world be happily governed," writes More, " . . . nor [will] the body politic be brought again to a good habit, as long as property remains."[2]

Campanella does with 17th century Naples what More did with 16th century England. The workers' democracy of Campanella's "City of the Sun" contrasts with the Neapolitan life where, according to the author himself, only 20 percent of the population was working, and doing so under conditions of exhaustion. His utopia, like More's, homologizes ethics with social and economic justice, the non-existence of servility, and an order where the State's action coincides with the will of civil society: "In the City of the Sun . . . it only falls to each one to work for about four hours every day," writes Campanella. "It is not the custom to keep slaves. . . . But with us, alas! it is not so."[3]

But the utopia of the Renaissance is more than an objection to modernity. It positively values scientific progress and knowledge. In it, the Renaissance utopians navigate by their epoch's compass. The "City of the Sun" is culturalist from the very bases of its architecture: it is composed of concentric circles, and within its walled fortress are engraved all scientific knowledge, all the discoveries and all the technical achievements available at that time. Bacon's utopia shares with Campanella's and More's the Renaissance exaltation of knowledge, brought to the extreme of covering the whole map of his ideal city. There, the idea that utopia is, after all, the maximum threshold of culture and that it contains all the cognitive memory of history. The words of one of the inhabitants of his New Atlantis are eloquent in this respect: "We maintain a trade, not for gold, silver, or jewels, nor for silks, nor for spices, nor for any other commodity of matter, but only for God's first creature, which was light; to have light, I say, of the growth of all the parts of the world."[4]

Utopia not only emphasizes the absent but also the repressed. Campanella speaks of the possibilities of freeing man from enslaving labor. Rousseau is only opposed to science when it is translated into techniques of domination. The gap between imaginary construction and existing order is but one moment in utopia. The other moment is the gap between a present moment marked by repressed possibilities, and potential future of freed possibilities. The critical function of utopic construction is therefore given in order to remake the repressed under the sign of the new.

Descriptive Force, Normative Force

Utopia is a bounded concept and a useful tool: it is at once immanent and transcendental regarding the era in which it is conceived. If it describes that which doesn't exist and cannot exist, by way of its extreme construction it facilitates the comprehension of that which does exist, and it deduces orientations for change based on this comprehension. Franz Hinkelammert has shown the transcendental character of the utopic construction and the dangers implied in forgetting that utopia is only this: an impossibility that orients and permits apprehension of the possible. "The framework of the possible is uncovered anew, through the imagination and through the conceptualization of the impossible. One who doesn't dare conceive the impossible will never discover the possible. The possible can be visualized only by submitting the impossible to the criteria of feasibility."[5] But while a political order or an ideology "doesn't manage to discern abundance as a possibility towards which one never advances in terms of an empirical progress in time, such abundance is simultaneously blinding and illuminating. It's impossible to be pragmatic without our realizing the transcendental character of such conceptualized abundance, and without our falling into the illusion of wanting to carry them out."[6] In this sense, utopia "is less a compensation for, than a complement to, existing reality," part of the social imagination that all societal reality acquires for its institution.[7]

That the *idea* of the republic is confused with the *ideal* republic shows us that in Plato the utopic construct already contains descriptive and normative force. Its force is descriptive, in the measure that in the ideal republic it is the "essence" of the republic as such, and on that account it allows for the passing of judgment on what is good and what is bad, what is desirable and what is undesirable.

On the ethical plane, utopia is normative, presenting or imagining the best that can be conceived and the most desirable. On the plane of knowledge, it is a limit, or a boundary, for the concept: it delimits the conditions of possibility for apprehending the existing social reality. From the platonic horizon, to think of the ideal republic is, then, to establish a paradigmatic referential frame on the basis of which the existing political reality becomes both intelligible to us and capable of giving us a sense of direction. Utopia, understood as an ideal order, turns into the real that is unrealizable, and into an impossibility that's more true than the possible. Utopic speculation is justified by its operating as a contrast: the ideal that it proposes makes evident what at present stands as unrealized or repressed.

Utopia as Mimesis, or, How the Square Root of X Squared is Not Equal to X

The utopic construction is reduction and potency. Both operations constitute complementary moments of a single construction.

Reduction underlines an aspect or potential within reality, which is only partially given in its deeds. The utopic construction thus turns over the real in order to rescue that which it considers more desirable and more promissory of reality, isolating it from all exogenous factors or elements that could distort, sully, or neutralize its potency. This implies that each utopia privileges a determinate aspect of reality: the neoliberal utopia privileges the market, and in order to do so isolates it from all "contaminating" elements. The developmentalist utopia does the same thing with the Planning State, the communitarian utopia with people's vocation for solidarity, the socialist utopia with socialized production, and the futurist utopia with the substitution of human labor by machine labor.

"Potency," in the sense of making something happen, and to raise exponentially, and to universalize, magnifies what was previously recovered in reduction: potency reconstructs a social universe different from the present one, where the element that the reduction has privileged grows and multiplies. In this way, in the neoliberal utopia, the market is rampant: it's transparent everywhere, and in all cases the paradigm of perfect equilibrium is fulfilled. In the developmentalist utopia, for example, the Planning State assumes with efficiency all the functions liable to be assigned to it: to modernize the productive apparatus, to integrate all social sectors into the benefits of industrialization, to harmonize conflicts without any mishaps, to redistribute and create growth at the same time. In the communitarian utopia, the experience of self-managed community activists, which in reality yield dispersed and interstitial results, appear multiplied and consolidated to such a point that they permeate the entire social fabric with humanist, fraternal values, instead of values of solidarity. The futurist utopia, finally, universalizes the technological component that has previously isolated all social or political components. It doesn't thematize the organization of production or the assignment of resources, but only the productive potential of the machines that would redeem social struggles by way of an inexorable march towards the paradise of leisure.

This process of reduction-potency shows the form that utopia has for feeding on and creating fissures in reality. Obviously, the type of reduction—what is privileged in it—reflects determinate and often exclusionary options. The paradox rests on utopia's trying to reconcile the exclusionary, but the reduction that operates in the utopic construction tends, intrinsically, to exclude by way of privileging one or another element of reality.

If one takes the utopic construction as a narrative with the double operation of reduction and potency, the functions of utopia show its fundamental ambiguity. As an *instrument of intelligibility* with regard to the real, utopia permits us a more penetrating but also more arbitrary vision of reality. It puts into relief potentialities that are contained or latent in reality, but channeled in a directionality that outlines it with a specific prism. As the *horizon of normativity*, utopia serves as a directional reference while departing from a perception that is, at the same time, a wager. The perception that serves as its base privileges certain elements to the detriment of others, and from there establishes an orientation that blocks off or sidesteps other possible orientations. In this way, utopia simultaneously opens a horizon of meaning for action, and limits that same horizon in a specific sense.

The Times of Utopia

For the Renaissance Utopians, utopia's time is simultaneously the present and its reverse. The gap is then given by space: it is in a remote place, habitually an unlocatable island where the narrator arrives by chance or error, where the scenario of an ideal society is mounted. In More's account, the testimony arrives by way of Raphael Hythlodaeus, an imaginary person who accompanies Amerigo Vespuccio in his sea voyages throughout the New World. In Campanella's utopia, the geographical place is uncertain, but the recourse of the testimony of an invented person, known as "the admiral," reappears. The New Atlantis, by Francis Bacon, is a similar case. To this spatial indetermination is added the fact that these utopias appear to us as timeless societies that have resisted and are unscathed by the battering of time. An unmistakable (and unmistakably platonic) feature of these utopias is their incorruptibility: history doesn't diminish these ideal societies. The ideal is united with what preexists and endures.

This image proposes that the challenge of utopia isn't only its plausibility, but also its sustainability. This is the problem that in the past century, the experience of the Paris Commune left open and unresolved, just as a multitude of ephemeral, small-scale experiences also did. Thus the importance of the dimension of temporality in the utopic invention. The problem of the utopic is, then, as much the unsustainable as the unrealizable. Plato already introduced the problem with the requirement of incorruptibility for the ideal republic.

The Desirable and the Unchangeable

Utopia is, then, the image of a desirable, durable order. But this poses a dilemma difficult to resolve: the durable becomes utopia in a static order; and between the static, the inalterable and the closed-off, the borders are diffuse. It's not accident, then, that the hell that Huxley depicts in his Brave New World would have a certain resonance with Campanella's City of the Sun. Each presents a compact universe in which individual happiness rests in everyone's having been programmed for their desires to coincide with what society and the State expect from them. No movement is possible there.

In this regard, it turns out to be symptomatic that the accounts of More and Campanella would be unfinished, apparently wanting to recuperate in their form the openness that their contents deny. This is because the problem of utopias is that the finished description of an ideal order is turned into the ideal description of a finished order. For a utopia to endure, there should be nothing lacking, and no detail can be allowed to escape from the description. But the resistance, in More as in Campanella, to closing the account can be interpreted as the resistance to constructing a closed utopia. This resistance isn't present in the less democratically inspired Plato. On the contrary, if in More utopia is fundamentally a democracy that persists and is incorruptible, in Plato democracy is a type of corruptible government, *par excellence*. Incorruptibility in the Greek philosopher therefore doesn't come up against the practical difficulties of pluralism and the will of the people.

This doesn't mean that the Renaissance utopias are distinguished by respect for individual autonomy or by a vocation for the liberty of citizens. Far from it. They all show, to a greater or lesser degree, the force of a Law that constrains the bodies of the citizens: it restricts spatial displacement, organizes the work of each one, and regulates sexuality. The same incorruptibility that they award to the utopia that they invent obliges them to insert into it an inflexible normativity. The durability of a model of society across time would require the direct coercion of all that menaces stability. It might well require totalitarian conditioning so that the will of the majority would be made to coincide with that of the status quo, just as individual desires would be made to coincide with public institutions, and subjective necessities with their objective satisfaction.

Utopia and Openness

The expectation of a definitive conciliation of individual aspirations, social organizations, and political decisions doubtless pierces utopic thinking as an extreme image. But this compulsion for conciliation is confused with the eschatological, and culminates in imaginary hermetic constructions such as Bacon's and Campanella's, or in ideal systems where cohesion is achieved by way of rigorous disciplinary conditioning, as with Plato. Even in the passionate utopias such as the phalansteries of Fourier, the regimentation of life is quite scrupulous and controls the body of each individual within the community.

The objection of neoliberal positivism to the utopic element of political doings is born from this normative force (or "constructivism") that utopia exercises and that is susceptible to being transformed in the coercion of individuals. This only happens, nevertheless, when the utopic construction becomes a dogma, and when its impossible quality is forgotten and actions are oriented as if the realization of a utopia were part of a strategic program. Curiously, it's precisely the neoliberals who deserve this reproach. Franz Hinkelammert has shown how the concept of perfect equilibrium, in neoclassical theories and in neoliberal ideology, is a "bounded" concept or a utopic construction; he also shows how the very defenders of neoliberalism confuse the transcendental function of utopia with its practical function, and fall into a kind of normativity that to them seems morally inadmissible.[8] This is one of the deepest contradictions in the neoliberal attack in Latin America: if on the one hand it denounces the totalitarian potential of the statist or Leftist Utopias, on the other hand its own crusade-like character is evidenced in the fact that it has resorted to violent military dictatorships in order to impose itself, and to conquer the physical and ideological resistence of sectors opposed to the utopia of the market.

The idea that utopia operates restrictively on reality, exerting a coercive force on individual will and limiting the recreation of alternatives, is an objection that deserves to be considered, not in order to disqualify utopic thinking, but in order to widen it, opening it up. The necessity of an open utopia exists, a utopia capable of continually reformulating itself, but which would not on that account be diluted into efficiency or impotence.

How to open the discourse of development to those open utopias without ceasing to recognize, in turn, social necessities that require collective attention? How to make utopia a normative horizon capable of effecting practice in a transformational direction, but which instead of becoming a force of coercion constitutes a force of liberation? These questions become more pertinent the more a participatory democracy, creative and capable of transforming itself, is revalued as a desirable order. In Latin America, an intercultural utopia can operate as a liberating referent, in contrast with the coercive character of past utopias that have reproduced, under various forms, the compulsion to negate the other—this other who is Native

American, mixed-blood, Black, a peasant, marginalized in the city, part of the informal economic sector, a woman, born out of wedlock, a domestic worker. This very intercultural utopia can simultaneously combine, on the basis of a criteria of openness and heterodoxy that suggests mestizaje/ racial mixture (in the best sense), an ideal of participatory democracy, of solidarity extended in the overcoming of poverty and socioeconomic exclusion, and a utopia of communication that provides widespread access to symbolic interchange by way of the culture industry.

By Way of Corollary: Determined But Not Closed

Utopia is a factual impossibility, absolutely desirable, that serves as an orienting horizon to frame the intelligibility of the real and to make patent the potentially repressed. As an imaginary construction, it's the expression of a desire, not just any desire, but a collective desire for a collective order. Just as it bestows meaning, it sets limits on what is desired. If on one side it grants contents, on the other side it marks the terrain of possible contents. This ambiguity is intrinsic to utopia.

Facing the anticonstructivist argument, which emphasizes the coercive or narrowing effect of utopias, one possible response is to renounce the utopic construction. But this renunciation is also the renunciation of a societal identity and intelligibility. Because in utopia, society "encounters as an initial investiture of the world and of society itself with a 'final sense' of life, by way of which people recognize and affirm themselves as a collective entity. This self-creation of society as collective life is, in a matter of speaking, the 'function' of utopia."[9] Utopia is the other face of the foundational myth: a social image that motivates reciprocal recognition between citizens of the same social body.

Another possible response involves renouncing utopias with contents. Utopia, then, is a formal referent that doesn't specify ends. It determines less what to do than how to do it. In this way it maintains an open as well as indeterminate character. Such is the case with *the utopia of consensus, the utopia of transparency,* and *the utopia of the perfectly representative.*

Here we confront the challenge of devising utopias which are open but not indeterminate. Social imaginary, normative horizon, transcendental referent, mystifying-demystifying: in any case, utopic production is currently passing through the ambiguous situation of being simultaneously indispensable and indefensible. Indispensable, because the magnitude of the crisis and the lack of shared projects makes even more urgent a horizon that, although utopic, restores personal experience to hope; because the litany of social theory, the death of *the* truth and the multiplication of interpretative methods and models require referents that are capable of orienting the projects of knowledge with *meaning* and new values. Indispensable because the social image or self-perception pierces such uncertainty that collective identity and intelligibility are threatened from various flanks, and utopic invention provides dreams to share, fantasies on which to ground intersubjectivity, ideals capable of restoring the terrain of dialogue.

That utopic plenitude would make sense doesn't imply that it operates reductively on the real. Such a reduction is only necessary in utopias that are millenialist, fundamentalist, closed-off, or exclusive. To conceive utopia as the order where necessities are definitively met is also to conceive dystopia. Necessities are never met. Rather, they are ceaselessly set in motion. The "meta-necessities" of utopia would be Campanella's *City of the Sun* becoming the *Brave New World* of Aldous Huxley: a very efficient program for immobility, and for forgetting that there are necessities that demand realization, potentialities that deserve to be actualized. The absence of needs is the absence of movement, and life requires movement.

An open utopia requires a change of rationality, and its efficiency for promoting it is what makes a political practice out of utopic speculation. The utopic construct should rescue as means and ends attributes such as solidarity and participation, social identity and freedom, belonging and work, communication and affection, collective creativity and cultural diversity: these possess value in themselves and radiate effects which are desirable beyond themselves. The continual realization of necessities and the progressive actualization of potentialities is, simultaneously, a road and a utopia. Today, to actualize this integrating rationality is a crucial challenge, because it implies breaking with the industrialist supposition to which capitalisms as well as real socialisms have been heir: namely, that only a highly industrialized society can begin by freeing human potentials.

Crisis closes off the future from the unfeasibility of the present. Vulnerability, precariousness, and the high degree of conflict in our peripheral societies corrode the will towards utopian constructs. Utopias that until the recent past ruled social projects of modernization have lost credit and popular legitimacy. Integrating modernization showed, for exogenous reasons and endogenous causes, little capacity for integration. The crisis swept away the last dreams of homogenous and constant progress.

What remains, as meaning and contents of utopia, for the Latin American periphery? The answer could well be posed as the reverse of the question: what remains to our precarious and tense realities if we cannot make them stand out, in a horizon of meaning capable of transcending that same precariousness and tension? Our region is stocked with myths, dispersed elements, the fragments of encounters, partial overflowings, informal interstices through which fragments of fantasy that are born or survive thread their way. One vein, not new but very much our own, would be to assume a mestizaje capable of *negating the negation of the other,* and to open the repressed abundance of intercultural riches inscribed in our history. Between literature, landscape, culture, the partial rationalization of life, and the certain dream of democratic coalitions, utopia can and must be produced. Utopia in order to reread crisis and utopia to split it open. Utopia, in order to restock with meaning what administrative rationality (imposed in the adjustment, in Mephistophelian deals regarding external credits, in the worthless composure of the utterly hopeless) has previously despoiled. Utopia that would not necessarily be universal, rational, western. But neither would it be reduced to a bucolic purism that in a short period of time would reflect the heterogeneity of our continent. Utopia that reduces, that mixes, that hybridizes, that combines and recombines anew the scarcity of the present in order to suggest the plenitude of the future.

Utopia that is both a factual impossibility and a cultural necessity, a political challenge and threat, dreams to trick both integration and the apocalypse.

Notes

1   Cepaur, *Desarrollo a Escala Humana: Una opción para el futuro.* Development Dialogue, special number (Dag Hammarskjöld Foundation, 1986), 9.

2   Sir Thomas More, Part 1, *Utopia.* Trans. Ralph Robynson [1551, 1901]. NY: The Colonial Press, 1901. 11 May 2001 ⟨http://www.dholliday.com/tmore/utopia001.htm⟩

3   Tommaso Campanella, *City of the Sun.* Trans. T. W. Halliday [1885]. NY: The Colonial Press, 1901. 11 May 2001 ⟨http://eserver.org/fiction/city-of-the-sun.txt⟩.

4   Sir Francis Bacon, *The New Atlantis* [1627]. 11 May 2001. ⟨http://www.sirbacon.org/links/newatlantis.htm⟩

5   Franz Hinkelammert, *El realismo en política como arte de lo posible* (Santiago de Chile: FLASCO, 1984), 11.

6   Hinkelammert, *El realismo,* 13–14.

7 Norbert Lechner, *El consenso como estrategia y como utopía* (Santiago de Chile: FLASCO, 1983), 21.

8 In this respect see Franz Hinkelammert, *Crítica de la razón utópica* (San José de Costa Rica: Colección Economía-Teología, 1984).

9 Norbert Lechner, *El consenso como estrategia y como utopía* (Santiago: FLACSO, 1983), 18.

Index

Adorno, T. A., 57, 59, 60, 61, 63, 65, 73, 74, 75 nn.1, 14, 92 n.13, 126. *See also* Critical theory; Frankfurt School

Alienation, xii, xiii, 15, 39, 44–45, 63, 64, 65; capitalist, 2; notion of, 74; of work, 62, 82

Apocalypse, 34, 37; and apocalyptic thought, 30, 36, 44. *See also* Disenchantment

Authoritarianism, ix, 48, 62; Authoritarian State, 61

Autonomy, 45, 60, 63, 68, 83, 85, 98, 149; ideals of, ix; local, 139. *See also* Emancipation

Bacon, F., 145, 148. *See also* Utopian thought

Campanella, T., 144, 145, 148, 149. *See also* Utopian thought

Capitalism, xiv, 15, 17, 18, 25, 27, 38, 83, 94, 113, 134, 144, 152; capitalist modernization, 98; financial, 35 n.5, 38, 113; peripheral-dependent, 144

CEPAL, xiii, xiv, 84; CEPALism, xvi, xix n.1, 119; ECLAC, 99, 116 n.4

Citizenship, 38, 52, 67, 69, 139; and citizens, 47, 151. *See also* Democracy

Civil society, 67, 68, 87, 95, 97, 98, 99, 101, 103, 105, 112, 113, 114, 115, 144

Coercion, 56, 64, 71, 82, 87, 150. *See also* Repression

Communication, 38, 77, 79, 126, 152; globalization, 21; revolution, 38; horizontal, 69; social, 33. *See also* Mass communication

Complexity, 79, 87, 89, 90, 98, 114

Conflict, 67, 103–107, 111, 136, 147, 152

Consensus, 95, 96, 99, 100, 115, 151

Consumption, 22, 23, 30, 40, 62, 84, 108; habits, 110

Crisis, xi–xviii, 86–90, 120, 124, 132, 135, 137, 142, 143, 152, 153; of governability, 106, 114, 115; of intelligibility, xvi, 65, 119, 121, 122, 136, 147, 151, 152; of organicity, xvii, 119, 120, 122; of paradigms, 122, of the Planning State, 103–114; of the State, 94–116, 136, 147, 151, 152

Critical theory, 55–58, 60, 61, 63, 68, 70, 71, 73–75. *See also* Critical thought

Critical thought, 57–59, 62, 67, 69; Criticism, 36, 56–61, 64–67, 69, 70, 71, 74, 77, 82, 84, 135; Critique, 62, 64, 71, 73, 81. *See also* Critical theory

Culture, 14, 17, 26, 27, 32, 33, 34, 42, 49, 50, 57, 69, 70, 71, 87–89, 92 n.11; cultural change, 7, 49; cultural consumption, 17, 23, 31, 34; of death, 27–30, and fundamentalism, 26; cultural hegemony, 48, 81–83; cultural industry, xiii, xv, xvi, 4, 17, 20, 30, 38, 44, 63, 70, 99, 151; subcultures, 28, 29, 30; of survival 31. *See also* Diversity; Identity

Decentralization, 18, 32, 67, 85, 87

Democracy, xiii, xv, 1, 14, 23, 26, 30, 32, 67, 69, 84, 85, 87–89, 131, 132, 144, 150, 151; democratic culture, 32, 89; democratic order, 68, 71; democratization, viii, xv, 32, 69, 106, 120, 126. *See also* Citizenship

Development, ix, 5–7, 22, 23, 25, 26, 28, 31, 32, 35 n.1, 36, 38, 41, 56, 62, 64, 65, 67, 70, 72, 78, 86, 97, 104–106, 123, 125, 130, 133, 134, 137, 139; alternative, xv, 128; another, 71–74; changing style of, 82–88; crisis of, 94–96; discourse, xi–xviii, 11 n.2, 23, 35 n.1, 63, 66, 119, 120, 130–134; model, xvi, 72, 90, 121; endogenous, 39; and homogenization, 80; individual, 19, 20; new sensibilities of, 136; planning of, 110–114; styles of, 4, 9, 120

Dialectic, 50, 51, 58, 60, 65; dialectical negation, 57, 58; dialectical thought, 57, 58

Directionality, 132, 133, 135, 137, 139, 147; historical, 129, 130

Discourse, viii, 19, 24, 25, 34, 36, 37, 44, 53, 65, 69, 126, 137; public, 102; of revolution, 135; of the social scientist, 121, 122

Disenchantment, vii, ix, xvii, xviii, 1, 28, 31, 34, 45, 66, 69, 137, 138; culture of, 3, 11; discourse of, 122; disenchanted, 14, 15, 36, 38, 81. *See also* Apocalypse

Disintegration, 26, 37–38, 65. *See also* Fragmentation

Diversity, viii, xiii, xv, 6, 9, 10, 31, 32, 33, 80, 82, 83, 84, 85, 89; diversification, 22, 23, 79, 111, 120, 121; cultural, 21, 31, 152

Domination, 49, 50, 56, 58, 63, 64, 71, 74, 99, 145; dominant culture, 57, 70; dominant rationalities, 43, 70, 74, 85

Education, 19, 72, 80, 82, 98, 130

Emancipation, viii, 2, 15, 16, 17, 30, 35 n.4, 58, 60, 64, 68, 74, 78, 79, 89; collective emancipation, 8, 63; mass, 26, 63, 64; redemption, xii, 2, 10, 15, 64. *See also* Autonomy; Liberation; Revolution

Enlightenment, xvii, xviii, 60, 62, 69, 80, 100, 122, 123, 124, 137; reason, 128–132; rationality, 124; utopia, 102. *See also* Critical theory

Equity, xv, 90; equitable distribution, 87; social, xiv, 32, 84. *See also* Redistribution

Ethnocentrism, 81, 83, 84, 90; and ethnic groups, 108; and ethnic minorities, 12 n.2, 72

Everyday life, 5–9, 15, 18, 68, 74

Exclusion, xi, xii, 20, 23, 26, 28, 64; excluded, 6, 7, 8, 12 n.2, 20–22, 28, 29, 32, 33, 108; social and socioeconomic, 26, 151

Fragmentation, 1, 17, 23, 30, 32, 38, 96, 103–109, 113, 114, 121; social and socio-cultural, xv, 3, 4, 9, 25, 107, 115;

and structural heterogeneity, 82, 83, 90, 95, 120, 139. *See also* Disintegration
Frankfurt School, 55, 56, 58–63, 65, 69, 71, 73, 74, 75 n.16, 85, 126. *See also* Critical theory; Adorno, T. A.; Horkheimer, M.; Marcuse, H.
Freedom, x, 57, 58, 59, 63, 64, 65, 78
Fundamentalism, 24–27, 33, 34, 90

Globalization, 4, 10, 22, 24, 27, 36, 70, 89; global communication, 17, 83; global order, 113; global system, 108
Government, 96, 104, 114, 116, 142, 143, 149
Governability, 109
Grassroots, 68, 71; communities, viii; organizations, ix, 88

Habermas, J., 68
Hegemony, 27, 43, 73, 90, 104, 122, 143; and culture, 108; hegemonic order, 74
Heller, A., 76 n.21, 92 n.11, 117–118 n.15
Hinkelammert, F., 145, 150
History, ix, 37, 39, 42, 60, 66, 79, 80, 97, 129, 139, 145; direction of, 64, 78; discourse of, 137; reason of, 136
Horkheimer, M., 57, 59, 60, 61. *See also* Critical theory, Frankfurt School

Identity, x, 4, 5, 39, 40, 71, 72, 79, 137, 151, 152; collective, xviii, 68, 88, 152; cultural, 5, 70, 84, 121, 131; and identification, 32, 33, 42, 56, 57; social, 23. *See also* Culture
Ideology, xiv, xviii, 18, 27, 49, 50, 56, 58, 59, 66, 70, 94, 97, 145; hegemonic, xv, 79–82; of progress, xii; pro-market, 131
Individualism, 8, 9, 20, 27, 80, 82, 83, 143
Informal sector, xiv, 5, 37, 39, 91 n.9, 107, 108, 109, 120
Instrumental rationality, 18–21, 27, 29, 30, 31, 84; capitalist, 27; instrumentalization, 19–21, 71; planning, revolution, and, 124–128. *See also* Instrumental reason
Instrumental reason, 19–21, 30, 32, 33,

61–63, 66, 68, 75 n.14, 125–128, 144; critique of, 71–74. *See also* Instrumental rationality
Integration, xiii, 2, 3, 5, 6, 9, 10, 11, 12 n.2, 23, 24, 37, 38, 65, 66, 79, 80, 82, 98, 99, 100, 108, 109; integratd, 20, 21, 29, 33, 36, 41, 46; social integration, xiv, 17, 21, 24, 28, 29, 32, 33, 37, 38, 84, 98, 108, 109, 111
Intellectuals, xi, xii, xvi, 15, 27, 55, 62, 63, 65, 66, 125, 135; and reality, xviii; and revolution, 135–137; roles of, xvii

Lechner, N., 92 n.11, 120
Left, 11 n.1, 120, 125, 126, 128, 134, 135; leftist intellectuals, xii
Legitimacy, 95, 96, 97, 99, 105, 106, 114, 115, 152; crisis of, 94, 95; legitimated power, 101; political, 96, 124; social, 85, 87; of state planning, 95
Liberalism, 27, 78, 81. *See also* Market(s)
Liberation, xii, xiii, 5, 15, 16, 59, 60, 64; mass, 5. *See also* Emancipation, Revolution
Lyotard, J. F., 78. *See also* Postmodernism

Manipulation, 50, 58, 69, 70–72
Marcuse, H., 56, 58–61. *See also* Frankfurt School
Market(s), xviii, 10, 14, 15, 18, 27, 29, 33, 38, 42–44, 48, 67, 68, 87, 89, 99, 102, 127, 128, 132, 143, 146, 147, 150; cultural, 8, 34; globalization of, 4, 36; hegemony, 92 n.10; ideology, 17, 82, 83, 84, 85, 122; rationalization of, xii; and social fragmentation, 30–32
Marxism, xvi, 48, 62, 69, 78, 82, 119
Masses, xvii, 14, 16, 23, 30, 32, 38, 66, 80, 97, 122, 143, 144; mass society, 37
Mass communication, 26, 63; mass media, 19, 25, 126; means of, 31. *See also* Communication
Medina Echavarría, J. 104, 116 n.7, 117 n.11
Mega-actor, 99, 100, 101, 111, 113, 114, 135

Meta-actor, 99, 100, 101, 106, 114, 115, 135

Metanarratives, 60, 65, 70, 78, 79, 119, 120; crisis of, 122; and narratives, viii, 11 n.1, 44, 45, 49, 53, 69, 147. *See also* Modernity, Modernization, Progress

Modernity, xi, 25, 32, 39, 40, 41, 45, 60, 70, 75 n.14, 83, 85, 88, 89, 122, 124, 143, 144; crisis of, 77; critique of, 77–81, 128–132

Modernization, x, xi, xiv, 4, 11 n.2, 14, 16, 17, 20, 25, 27, 40, 41, 78, 80, 84, 86, 89, 90, 94, 95, 97, 98, 100, 101, 131, 132, 133, 134, 139, 140 n.6, 144, 152; alternatives forms of, 67–71; crisis of, 104–114, 120–128; paradigm, 84

More, T., 144, 148, 149. *See also* Utopian thought

Negative thought, 36, 55–71, 75; negation, 58–65, 72, 73; negativity, 58, 59, 72. *See also* Critical thought

Neoliberalism, xvi, 15, 48, 77, 78, 81, 84, 89, 128, 150; neoliberals, 81, 84, 92 n.10, 114, 127, 128, 134, 150; neoliberal ideology, 15, 150; neoliberal utopia, 146, 147; postmodern, 83. *See also* Privatization

Paradigms, xvii, 67, 77–80, 83, 84, 102, 140 n.2, 147; change in, 89–90; crisis of, 77–80, 119, 120, 124; of the Planning State, 111

Paradox, 37, 38, 39, 40, 41, 43–45, 49

Participation, viii, ix, xv, 12 n.2, 31, 32, 85, 111, 128, 134, 152; collective, 30, 68; community, 33, 88; political, 23, 32, 139; social, 67, 84, 87, 89

Periphery, 43, 44, 63, 83, 153; peripheral capitalism, 90; peripheral societies, 152

Personal development, xiii, xv, 33, 44, 45

Planning, 8, 37, 66, 83, 85–87, 89, 90, 92 n.15, 116 n.7, n.8, 117 n.10, n.11, 122, 137, 139, 140 n.8, 143; crisis of, 95–97, 123–126; and instrumental reason, 125–128; paradigm of, 100–102, 111; and

revolution, 129–137. *See also* Planning State

Planning State, 1, 94–116, 117 n.13, 120, 123, 127, 146, 147; and revolution, 128–132; as utopia, 132–136. *See also* Planning

Planners, 69, 70, 95, 96, 100, 101, 103, 123, 124, 133, 137, 138. *See also* Planning, Planning State

Plato, 133, 134, 144, 146, 148, 149; Platonism, 57

Pluralism, xviii, 69, 89, 138, 149

Politics, viii, 14, 24, 27, 32, 45, 47, 48, 49, 51, 52, 66, 68, 71, 74, 77, 80, 82, 86, 88, 89, 131, 135, 142–144; political culture, 11 n.1; political discourse, xii, 15, 19, 26, 96; political parties, 87–89, 109; political power, 100, 120, 136; political system, xiii, xv, 37, 68

Poor, 22–24

Popper, K., 133, 134

Postmodernism, 77–90, 92 n.11, 134; postmodern culture, 92 n.11; postmodern debate, 88, 89, 90, 121; postmodern discourse, 79, 81, 82, 122, 138, 139; and postmodernists, 78, 79, 128; postmodern narrative, 81, 83; and postmoderns, 5, 65, 80, 90, 134; postmodern tribes, 46. *See also* Postmodernity

Postmodernity, 30, 65, 80, 86, 123. *See also* Postmodernism

Poverty, xii, 15, 20, 23, 33, 89, 109, 122

Power, 48, 50, 51, 62, 63, 70, 73, 74, 80, 83, 100, 104, 105, 107, 123, 125, 136, 137, 143; rationalization of, 125; struggle for, 126. *See also* State

Privatization, viii, xi, 14, 18, 21–24, 82, 131; privatizing secularization, 24. *See also* Neoliberalism

Progress, ix, x, 4, 5, 11 n.2, 23, 59, 70, 78, 79, 80, 100, 102, 109, 128, 129, 132; directionality of, 100; of freedom, 57; and modernity, 78, 79, 80; rationality of, 70. *See also* Modernity, Metanarrative, Modernization

Projects, ix, 5, 8, 11 n.1, 41, 50; collective

projects, viii, 3, 4, 65, 138, 143; projects of modernization, xvii

Public, 29, 54; public space, 68, 69, 107, 109

Quality of life, 40–41, 44, 45, 126

Radical change, 4, 11 n.1, 47, 49, 51, 55, 125, 135. *See also* Revolution

Rationality, 74, 79, 80, 85, 105, 130; communicational, 67, 68; crisis of, 122, 124, 137; of development, 39; dominant, 43, 71; formal, 60; of history, 80, 123; instrumental, 19, 24, 30, 31, 126, 127, 128; of modernity, 122, 123; technical, 24, 104, 133; technological, 25, 123, 124; totalizing, 120; utopian, 133. *See also* Rationalization

Rationalization, xii, 44, 60, 62, 63, 73, 125, 127, 130, 153; systemic, 63, 68, 70. *See also* Rationality

Redistribution, 82, 101, 105, 109, 126; policies, 110; redistributive struggle, 32; regressive, 37; social, 105, 127. *See also* Equity

Reification, 58, 59, 60, 62, 71. *See also* Alienation

Repression, 49, 50, 59, 63. *See also* Coercion

Resistance, 43, 68, 73, 74

Revolt, 47–54

Revolution, xii, xvii, xviii, 1, 11, 43, 48, 64, 65, 86, 122, 123, 138, 140 n.4; death of, 2–6, 15, 16; market, 92 n.10; revolutionary discourse, 125; social, xiii, 17, 122; socialist, xii, 15, 16, 122–37. *See also* Emancipation; Liberation; Radical change

Secularization, viii, 14, 16, 17, 18, 19, 25, 27, 32, 33, 65. *See also* Modernity

Social actors, 69, 82, 87, 100, 106, 110, 115, 116, 132; and social sectors, 95, 106, 107. *See also* Social fabric, Social movements

Social change, xi, xii, xvi, xvii, 15, 16, 69, 120, 123, 132, 136; social transforma-

tion, 73, 123; structural change, 6, 10, 106, 120, 123, 135

Social fabric, 31, 72, 87–89, 101, 107, 114, 115, 126, 132, 147. *See also* Social actors, Social movements

Socialism, 25, 36, 127–133, 143, 152; socialist criticism, 76 n.21. *See also* Revolution

Social knowledge, 122, 123, 132, 137; social reflection, 63, 121; social research, 74; social researchers, 73. *See also* Social science

Social mobility, 12 n.2, 22, 23, 28, 38

Social movements, ix, xv, 10, 47, 68, 69, 87–89, 132; new, xv, 68, 69, 72, 88, 139. *See also* Social actors, Social fabric

Social science, 78, 87, 89; crisis of, ix, xi, xvi–xviii, 66, 77, 78, 119–124; new paradigms of, 137–139. *See also* Social scientist, Social theory

Social scientist, 67, 68, 119, 120–124, 132, 137–139. *See also* Social science, Social theory

Social theory, 56, 64, 65, 66, 121, 152. *See also* Social Science, Social scientist

Solidarity, 16, 19, 22, 32, 33, 43, 108, 126, 128, 134, 139, 147, 151, 152

State, xiv, 80, 82, 83, 85, 87, 88, 90, 125, 140 n.3, 143; delegitimation of, ix, 94–115; populist, 102, 113, 120; postmodern critique of, 71; planning, x, xiv, xv, 82, 111, 122, 127–131; Statist narrative, 52. *See also* Power, Planning State

Subjectivity, x, 11, 48, 60, 69, 70, 89; Subject, ix, 2, 79, 81

Technological change, 78, 85, 89

Touraine, A., 93 n.17

Transnationalization, 5, 42, 108, 113

Underdevelopment, 39, 115, 122; underdeveloped countries, 43

Unmasking, 50, 51, 56, 63, 64, 70; unveiling, 58

Utopia, xiii, 10, 15, 17, 26, 27, 28, 47, 50, 52, 79, 85, 95, 114, 122, 126, 130–137,

140 n.8, 142–153; capitalist, 18; communitarian, 146, 147; and critical function, 144–146; critique of, 82; death of,
1, 3, 9, 24; developmentalist, 146, 147;
end of, 11 n.1; open, 149, 150–52; of
Planning State, 97–103; socialist, xi,
147; technocratic, 104; times of, 148. *See
also* Utopian thought
Utopian thought, 91 n.7, 142; crisis and,

142–144; utopian reason, 133–135, 140
n.7; utopianism, xi, xviii, 124, 135, 137;
utopianizing rationality, 124; utopic
construction, 145–147, 150, 151; utopic
thinking, 144, 150. *See also* Utopia

Violence, viii, x, 3, 6, 8, 25, 28–30, 32, 34,
42, 48, 99, 108; social, 33
Vulnerability, 44, 105, 112–115

Martín Hopenhayn is a consultant for the United Nations Economic
Commission for Latin America and the Caribbean (CEPAL).

Library of Congress Cataloging-in-Publication Data
Hopenhayn, Martín.
[Ni apocalípticos, ni integrados. English]
No apocalypse, no integration : modernism and postmodernism in
Latin America / Martín Hopenhayn; translated by Elizabeth Rosa
Horan and Cynthia Margarita Tompkins.
p. cm. – (Post-contemporary interventions) (Latin America in
translation/en traducción/em tradução)
Includes index.
ISBN 0-8223-2760-0 (cloth : alk. paper)
ISBN 0-8223-2769-4 (pbk. : alk. paper)
1. Latin America — Civilization — 1948–. 2. Latin America — Social
conditions — 1982–. 3. Latin America — Economic conditions —
1982–. I. Title. II. Series. III. Series: Latin America in translation/en
traducción/em tradução.
F1414.2.H62 2001   980.03′3 — dc21   2001040630